The People Dividend

*Leadership Strategies for Unlocking
Employee Potential*

Mike Horne, Ph.D.

The moral right of the author has been asserted

The Empire Publishers publishing
12808 West Airport Blvd Suite 270M Sugar Land, TX 77478

https://empirepublishers.co/about-us

Our books may be purchased in bulk for promotional, educational, or business use.
Please contact The Empire Publishers at +(844) 636-4576, or by email at support@theempirepublishers.com

First Edition September 2024

Dedication

I dedicate this book to every client, executive, leader, manager, and peer who has inspired me along this journey. Your insights, collaboration, and unwavering support have shaped my understanding of leadership and its profound impact on individuals and organizations. I am genuinely grateful for the opportunity to learn from each of you and to contribute to a shared vision of unlocking potential together. This dedication extends to those who have shared their experiences and vulnerabilities with me, allowing for candid conversations about the joys and struggles of leadership. Your stories have illuminated leaders' diverse challenges and reaffirmed my belief in the transformational power of empathy and connection.

I also extend my heartfelt gratitude to my teachers and mentors, whose wisdom and guidance have been invaluable throughout my journey. Your encouragement and belief in my potential have inspired me to strive for excellence and confidently embrace challenges. To my students, thank you for your curiosity and passion for learning; you remind me daily of the transformative power of education. Together, we cultivate an environment of exploration and growth. I hope to continue nurturing your aspirations and dreams as you embark on your paths of leadership and discovery.

Lastly, I want to honor the individuals who, though they may not hold titles or positions of power, exhibit extraordinary leadership in their everyday lives. From inspiring their colleagues to nurturing the talents of others, these unsung heroes remind us that leadership transcends formal roles. You embody the essence of resilience and authenticity, and your commitment to fostering growth—both in yourself and in those around you—truly unlocks the potential we seek in our workplaces and communities.

Table of Contents

A Note to the Reader

Dear Reader,

Thank you for picking up *The People Dividend: Leadership Strategies for Unlocking Employee Potential*. My career has been deeply rooted in global corporate human resources (HR), organization development (OD) leadership, and executive coaching. I am passionate about empowering aspiring leaders, executives, and teams to excel, expand their influence, and enhance both their personal and professional effectiveness.

Since beginning my coaching journey, I've had the privilege of guiding numerous leaders and teams across various sectors. Collaborating with respected organizations has underscored my dedication to nurturing immediate improvements and fostering sustainable progress. As the host of *The People Dividend Podcast*, I share diverse perspectives and inspiring stories aimed at redefining human capital management. This podcast, recognized in the top 10% globally, makes me incredibly proud. In 2021, I published my first book, *Integrity by Design: Working and*

Living Authentically.

My nearly thirty years of experience in HR and OD included significant roles such as head of Human Resources for Gilead Sciences' research division, global leader of talent and development for Brocade, head of Organization Development for Genentech (a division of Roche Pharmaceuticals), and global leader for Organization Development at Marriott International. These roles have greatly influenced my approach to leadership and organizational dynamics.

Currently, I serve as the program director for graduate programs in human resources and leadership at Golden Gate University in San Francisco. I hold a doctorate in Human and Organizational Systems from Fielding Graduate Institute, a Master's in Human Resources and Organization Development from American University, and a Bachelor of Science in Labor Relations from La Salle University. My coaching credentials, including Immunity to Change and Positive Intelligence Coaching certificates, further enhanced my ability to provide strategic guidance. Additionally, I've held board leadership roles with the Organization Development Network (ODN) and the *Organization Development Review*. My experience as a Peace Corps volunteer in the Solomon Islands has also profoundly shaped my path to service and leadership.

Through my experiences and achievements, I've established myself as a trusted authority on creating effective, humanistic workplaces. *The People Dividend* aims to share these insights, offering strategies and tools to unlock your team's full potential and create thriving, people-centered organizations.

Warm regards,

Mike

Preface

In the hectic world of modern business, amidst the relentless pursuit of targets and the constant flow of meetings, there lies an often overlooked truth so fundamental yet frequently ignored. It's the tale of untapped potential, of talent left to diminish. As an employee, I sometimes felt like a cog in the vast machinery of an organization where my potential was glossed over by the very people tasked with bringing out the best in me. As a manager, I was also guilty of overlooking the people right in front of me.

Like many, I entered the workforce fueled by ambition and the desire to make a meaningful contribution. Yet, it wasn't long before I encountered the stark reality that plagues countless workplaces: a culture of neglect towards the human element. Managers, caught up in the whirlwind of pleasing superiors, navigating their career trajectories, and ticking off task lists, often lose sight of their most pivotal role: nurturing the talent right before them.

This neglect isn't just an oversight; it's a systemic issue that erodes the very foundation of an organization. Poor managerial practices—failing to recognize achievements, not providing constructive feedback, or simply not listening—can diminish even the brightest and most resilient workers. Poor management contributes to teams and organizations where potential is squandered. The cost? A profound drag on the morale, productivity, and innovation of teams and organizations alike.

It's a narrative all too common yet deeply personal to me. I've lived through the disappointment of being invisible, of striving to contribute more only to confront barriers erected by those who should have been my mentors and champions. I know the frustration of having managers tell you that you're doing a good job when they don't have a clue what you are actually doing. But this story isn't unique to me—it echoes experiences shared by countless others across various sectors and job titles.

The tragedy in all this lies not in the complexity of the solution but in its simplicity. We don't need groundbreaking strategies or radical overhauls to address this oversight. The remedy lies in paying attention—to treat each employee with the respect, dignity, and kindness they deserve. This book was born from personal experience and a deep-seated belief in the power of change. It's a call to action for leaders, managers, and individuals at every level of an organization to awaken to the potential that lies within their reach—the people dividend.

Unlocking this dividend doesn't require magic; it demands a shift in perspective, a commitment to see beyond the numbers and tasks, and a recognition of the human beings driving the success of any enterprise. This book is your guide to making that shift and tapping into the immense value that has been there all along, waiting just beneath the surface.

The Problem

In the pressures of today's business environment, where agility and innovation are necessary for survival, a critical issue is lurking, undermining the potential of organizations worldwide. The problem isn't rooted in technology or market competition. Rather, the enemy is managers and leaders who don't know enough to care and respect others despite decades-long mantras that human capital is the most valuable asset. We are dealing with an endemic failure to invest adequately in people, leading to a cascade of people and culture challenges that jeopardize a firm's long-term sustainability and growth.

Recent studies paint a concerning picture of the current state of talent management and leadership. A 2023 report by Gallup revealed that a staggering 85% of employees are not engaged or actively disengaged at work, highlighting a glaring disconnect between workforce expectations and the reality of their professional environment.[1] Such disengagement is not merely a symptom of dissatisfaction but a demonstration of the prevalent inadequacies in leadership and management practices that fail to inspire, recognize, and develop the latent potential within their teams.

Furthermore, the same survey underscores the dismal

consequences of this disengagement on talent retention, with over one-third of the workforce considering new job opportunities at any given time. This revolving door syndrome, recently dubbed quiet quitting, not only incurs significant recruitment and training costs but also erodes institutional knowledge and disrupts team cohesion, further exacerbating the challenges organizations face in maintaining a competitive edge.

The figures are equally telling in terms of investment in people development. According to Bersin by Deloitte, only 25% of companies believe their leadership development programs add significant value, and just 24% consider their models "up to date" or "highly relevant."[2] Additionally, a McKinsey & Company report reveals that while over 90% of CEOs view leadership development as essential, only 10% think these programs have a substantial impact.[3,4] These discrepancies highlight a critical gap: recognizing the importance of people development does not translate into effective action and investment.

Poor team dynamics, often a byproduct of ineffective leadership, further compound these issues. In a recent *Harvard Business Review* article, Behnam Tabrizi, a consulting professor at Stanford University, wrote about why teams don't thrive.[5] He shared insights from a study indicating that nearly 75% of cross-functional teams are dysfunctional, failing on at least three of five criteria, including meeting a planned budget, staying on schedule, adhering to specifications, meeting customer expectations, and maintaining alignment with the company's goals. Such dysfunction squashes innovation and productivity and deteriorates workplace culture, making it challenging to attract and retain top talent.

The juxtaposition of recognizing the paramount value of people against the stark reality of insufficient action to mobilize this insight into a coherent, effective strategy represents a significant challenge for businesses today. The gap is not one of ignorance but a failure to act with a view toward people at the center or heart of an organization. Leadership and management, therefore, stand at a crossroads—between continuing down a path of minimum investment in their most important asset, people, or pivoting towards a future where the development, engagement, and retention of talent are central to business strategy, driving sustainable growth and success in an increasingly complex and competitive world.

The Purpose of the Book

The People Dividend is not just a book; it's a call to revolutionize the bedrock of business success. At its heart, this work is dedicated to a singular mission: transforming the way businesses perceive and manage their people. This book challenges the status quo, proposing a radical shift from viewing employees as mere cogs in the corporate machine to recognizing them as the core drivers of value creation and sustainable growth. It advocates for a paradigm where strategic people management transcends conventional boundaries, evolving into a practice of people-centered performance.

The concept of the people dividend is the substantial

return on investment that businesses can unlock through a strategic, people-focused strategy. This dividend manifests not merely in financial terms but holistically, encompassing improved employee engagement, heightened innovation, enhanced company reputation, and beyond. It posits that when organizations invest thoughtfully in their human capital—nurturing leadership skills, fostering inclusive cultures, and creating environments where every team member can thrive—these investments yield exponential returns. These returns are not limited to enhanced productivity or profitability alone; they extend to forging a resilient organizational fabric capable of weathering the challenges of the volatile, uncertain, complex, and ambiguous (VUCA) world we live in today.

The People Dividend dispels the myth that investing in people is a cost rather than a profit center. Through evidence, examples, and actionable insights, I will demonstrate how a people-centered strategy is fundamentally the most effective approach to unlocking the latent potential within organizations. It brings to the forefront the undeniable truth that people are not just part of the business equation—they are the equation.

This book is an essential roadmap for leaders, managers, human resources professionals, and indeed, anyone vested in an organization's success. It lays down the principles of strategic people management, illuminating a plan to achieve the people dividend through deliberate actions and mindset shifts. By prioritizing people and treating them with the respect, dignity, and the investment they deserve, businesses can enhance their operational outcomes and contribute to a more equitable, fulfilling, and viable future for all stakeholders.

Essentially, the people dividend seeks to inspire a movement towards people-centered performance, urging businesses to reimagine their system of human resource management. It is an invitation to begin viewing employees not as liabilities to be minimized but as assets to be maximized. This book is your guide to unlocking the full spectrum of benefits that come from truly valuing the people behind the profit, discovering along the way that the greatest dividend any organization can achieve is the loyalty, creativity, and excellence of its people.

How to Use This Book

The People Dividend: Leadership Strategies for Unlocking Employee Potential is a comprehensive guide for leaders committed to fostering humanistic values in the workplace. Through insights, advice, and success stories, this book emphasizes the importance of respect, dignity, inclusion, and integrity, demonstrating that investing in people leads to unparalleled business success.

While the book is structured to be read from start to finish, feel free to navigate the core ideas and strategies at your own pace. Each chapter builds on the principles of creating a human-centered workplace, valuing individualism, leveraging diversity, and leading with integrity to unlock the full potential of your team. Adopting these practices will prepare you to champion a future where human potential is at the heart of business growth and success.

Whether you're new to leadership or a seasoned professional, this book provides actionable insights that can be tailored to your unique organizational context. Dive in, explore the concepts, and implement the strategies that resonate most with you to create a thriving, people-centered workplace.

What You Can Expect to Gain by Investing Your Time in this Book

In *The People Dividend*, I invite you to embark on a transformative journey that will redefine the essence of your leadership and organizational success. By engaging deeply with the principles and strategies in this book, you stand to gain insights and tools that promise to elevate your methods of people management. What follows is a preview of the tangible benefits and expected outcomes you can anticipate.

Enhanced Company Culture

One of the foremost advantages of applying the concepts from this book is cultivating a vibrant, inclusive company culture. By embedding humanistic values at your organization's core, you will encourage an environment where respect, dignity, and integrity are espoused and lived experiences. This cultural shift enhances the workplace atmosphere and attracts and retains top talent, setting a solid foundation for long-term achievement.

Increased Employee Engagement and Satisfaction

The strategies discussed offer a roadmap to significantly improve employee engagement and satisfaction. By recognizing the individual value of each team member and investing in their growth and well-being, you will release a level of motivation and commitment that transforms how work is approached. Engaged employees are happier, more productive, creative, and willing to go the extra mile for the organization.

Boosted Productivity

At the heart of the people dividend is the notion that people-centered performance is the key to unlocking unprecedented productivity levels. Through chapters dedicated to building trust, encouraging open communication, and cultivating community, you'll discover practical ways to energize your teams and streamline operations. This book will equip you with the knowledge to remove barriers to productivity, ensuring that you and your organization operate at peak efficiency.

Elevated Profitability

The most compelling outcome of implementing the insights from this book is the direct impact on your bottom line. The people dividend conceptualizes employees as investments rather than expenses. By nurturing your human capital, you're enhancing their lives and driving profitability. Companies with happy and engaged employees typically report higher sales, better customer satisfaction, and improved financial performance.

A Roadmap for the Future of Work

Finally, *The People Dividend* offers a forward-looking

perspective, preparing you and your organization for the future of work. With trends leaning towards more human-centered business practices, this book provides the mindsets and frameworks needed to thrive in tomorrow's corporate environment. You will learn to anticipate changes, adjust leadership styles, and make strategic decisions that ensure you and your organization remain relevant and competitive.

By turning the pages of this book, you're not just acquiring knowledge; you're gaining a partner in your quest to create a profitable workplace that is purposeful and fulfilling for everyone involved. The principles and strategies within these chapters are more than theories—they are a call to action for anyone ready to lead with courage, compassion, and conviction. Welcome to the beginning of your organization's transformation towards procuring the people dividend—a testament to the power of investing in human potential.

Call to Action

As you stand at the precipice of change, ready to turn the pages of *The People Dividend,* I urge you to do so with an open heart and a mind willing to venture beyond the familiar boundaries of traditional people management. This book beckons you to envision and actively pursue a new paradigm where employees are realized as the most important investments of your organization. It's a call to elevate your leadership by recognizing the profound potential that lies within human-centered practices.

I challenge you to dismantle the old notions that have

limited the scope of what you believe is possible in workplace dynamics. Please look beyond the immediate cost implications to the substantial, long-term dividends a truly engaged, respected, and well-cared-for workforce can deliver.

Your employees are not robots in corporate machinery but the lifeblood of innovation, commitment, and business success. Their value transcends simple productivity metrics; they are the architects of your company's future, the creators of a workplace culture that can thrive amid the challenges and changes of the modern world.

"To handle yourself, use your head; to handle others, use your heart." This timeless wisdom, attributed to Eleanor Roosevelt, perfectly encapsulates the essence of the people dividend. It serves as a poignant reminder that the key to unlocking the full potential of our organizations lies not in spreadsheets and strategy documents alone but in the hearts and minds of the people we lead.

Imagine a workplace where every individual feels genuinely valued, where their contributions are recognized not just for the immediate benefits but for the lasting impact they have on the company's culture, reputation, and success. This is the heart of the people dividend—it's about seeing the human spirit that drives everything we do.

I hope you feel inspired and empowered to implement change when you finish the book. The path to achieving the people dividend in your organization may be challenging but will undeniably be rewarding. I encourage you to remember that the greatest returns come from investing in people. May your leadership journey be marked by courage, compassion, and an unwavering commitment to elevating those around you.

Chapter 1

The Human-Centered Workplace: Redefining Leadership

Have you ever worked with a boss who made you feel unstoppable? The kind of inspirational leader for whom you would have willingly ventured into uncharted territory? Leaders like these are unicorns in the world of work.

My own encounter was with a senior executive who cultivated an environment brimming with open dialogue, consistently upholding a policy of openness. He trusted me and encouraged me to speak up and stay involved. Regardless of the demands of his global responsibilities, he was always ready to listen to what I had to say. Sure, he wasn't thrilled with my work sometimes, and he told me so. Yet, his respect for me never wavered, and his interest in my perspectives was steadfast. Even on his off days, I never doubted that he cared.

In an era where organizational success is often measured solely in terms of financial performance and market share, the concept of people-centered performance emerges as a beacon for change, advocating for workplaces that prioritize human dignity, equity, and well-being. At its core, people-centered management is a system that seeks to harmonize organizational success, measured by financial and operational objectives, with the well-being of employees. It is rooted in the belief that businesses should operate in sustainable, ethical, and beneficial ways to all stakeholders—including society at large.

Delivering people-centered performance reshapes our understanding of the workplace, refocusing on the well-being and growth of every individual. It is rooted in theories pioneered by psychologists such as Abraham Maslow and Carl Rogers, emphasizing the importance of addressing human needs and advancing an environment that encourages individuals to realize their full potential. Additionally, Mary Parker Follett's groundbreaking work in management theory highlights the significance of collaborative leadership and the holistic integration of individual and organizational goals. By integrating the principles of people-centered performance in the workplace, organizational leaders, just like the one I described, nurture a culture where employees feel valued, understood, and empowered to contribute their best work.

The evolution of humanistic management and people-centered performance reflects the changing workplace and the increasing recognition of the importance of human values in business operations. These principles are more relevant than ever in fast-paced, digital, and often remote work environments. For example, a telling statistic from the World Health Organization highlights the economic toll of mental health conditions like depression and anxiety, costing the global economy about $1 trillion annually in lost productivity.[6] Human-centered methods are pragmatic strategies that directly contribute to the sustainability and profitability of businesses in the digitally connected world. These strategies and means offer an agenda for addressing the challenges of employee engagement, mental health, and the integration of work and personal life.

The development of people-centered performance stems partly from the evolving nature of the work environment, marking a critical shift towards honoring human values within business. Flexible work arrangements are one example of people-centered performance. Many companies in the technology sector (for example Dropbox, Slack, and Salesforce) have introduced policies that allow employees to choose where and when they work.[7] This flexibility might include remote work, flexible hours, compressed workweeks, or job sharing. These initiatives recognize employees' diverse needs and life circumstances and acknowledge that a one-size-fits-all strategy is no longer viable.

The shift that is underway reflects a growing awareness of the critical role that employee well-being plays in the broader context of organizational success. It draws from a wellspring of thought leadership in human resources (HR) and organization development (OD). I take personal inspiration from Charlie and Edie Seashore, Dick Beckhard,

Warren Bennis, and Peter Block, whose ideas and insights into organizational culture, leadership dynamics, and the essence of community in the workplace have been instrumental in shaping my strategy for people-centered performance management. By championing principles like transparency, dignity, and collective progress, people-centered management aligns organizational objectives with the sustenance of the individual, a model that is not only effective but ethically grounded.

In the vast expanse of management theories, the allure of humanistic management lies in its simplicity and profound impact. It isn't about reinventing the wheel but shifting the pendulum to place humanity at the core of organizational life. By emphasizing the value of each individual, this method seeks to create an environment where employees feel genuinely valued as human beings with unique needs, aspirations, and potential. The philosophy extends beyond mere productivity and efficiency; it's about nurturing organizational cultures that celebrate diversity and convey a deep sense of belonging.

The significance of people-centered management cannot be overstated, especially in an increasingly automated and technology-driven world. Amid many demands, it's easy for executives to lose sight of their most valuable asset—people. This management strategy reminds us that, even in the age of AI and robotics, the human element remains irreplaceable. It's about leveraging technology to enhance human work, not replace it, ensuring that progress never comes at the cost of well-being.

Reflecting on the principles of people-centered leadership also reveals a broader societal impact. It encourages organizational leaders to consider their role in the community and the environment, promoting sustainable practices and social responsibility. In this sense, the strategies you will learn in this book transcend workplace boundaries, contributing to a more just and compassionate world. It's an action-oriented testament to the power of placing people at the heart of business decisions. This strategy enriches employees' lives and promises long-term success and societal improvement.

Core Principles of People-Centered Leadership

The concept of people-centered performance requires a mental shift toward valuing human dignity, equity, and overall well-being within the corporate world and a departure from financial growth at all costs. I advocate for a blended approach where business success is achieved not at the expense of employees but through their growth and satisfaction. I am proposing an integrated framework where a corporation's financial objectives align seamlessly with the well-being of its people, asserting that a company's true success is measured not just by its balance sheets but also by its positive impact on its people and society.

The development of my approach is a direct response to the evolving dynamics of modern workplaces, characterized by their fast-paced nature, digitalization, and often, the physical distance between team members. It presents a set of principles tailored to meet contemporary challenges in employee engagement and the blurred lines between professional and personal life. The pioneers in this field have underscored the importance of cultivating corporate cultures that value community, transparency, and mutual respect, setting a standard for leadership that emphasizes the growth and development of individuals and teams.

At its essence, this is a call to return to basics—to recognize and nurture the human element in business operations. It suggests a shift towards viewing employees as integral stakeholders whose contributions extend beyond mere function. In an era dominated by technological advancement, this methodology is a vital reminder of the irreplaceable value of human insight, creativity, and connection. Through fostering an environment that prioritizes humanistic values, people-centered leadership lays the groundwork for enhancing organizational performance and making a meaningful contribution to global welfare.

To further encapsulate the essence of people-centered performance, it's essential to distill its guiding principles into actionable practices. Below are the key elements that organizations and their leaders can adopt to embody this management philosophy in daily operations. These practices enhance the workplace environment and contribute to employees' overall satisfaction and growth, thereby creating a great-place-to-work culture.

1. **Respect for the individual** underscores the importance of treating each employee as a person with unique needs, aspirations, and potential. It entails providing opportunities for personal and professional growth and recognizing the

intrinsic worth of each team member.

2. **The importance of community and belonging** highlights the value of creating a sense of connection and community within the organization. This principle advocates for an inclusive culture where everyone feels valued and part of a collective mission.

3. **Creating value through people** acknowledges that an organization's value lies in its human capital. This mode leverages employees' strengths, creativity, and innovation to drive organizational success.

4. **Leadership** plays a decisive role in aiding a humanistic culture. Leaders are not just figureheads but the embodiment of the values of empathy, transparency, and integrity. They set the tone for the organizational culture and influence how work gets done, thereby shaping overall success.

5. **Accountability and ethical considerations** are the bedrock of every successful organization. They ensure that goals are achieved in an equitable and just manner. This involves making decisions that are in the best interest of all stakeholders and upholding high ethical standards in every aspect of the business, thereby reinforcing a commitment to fairness and integrity.

6. **Empowering habitual learning and adaptation** underscores the recognition that an organization must encourage a culture of ongoing learning and flexibility to thrive. These principles advocate for creating opportunities for employees to acquire new skills, knowledge, and competencies that align with evolving industry trends and

organizational needs. It moves us from seeing people as replaceable to recognizing them as renewable assets.

7. **Practicing sustainability and social responsibility** broadens the scope of people-centered performance beyond the confines of the organization, urging businesses to take an active role in addressing global challenges. This principle underscores the importance of operating in a way that benefits the company and contributes positively to society. It calls for actions supporting sustainable development goals, reducing undesirable environmental footprints, enhancing community well-being, and aligning business operations with the broader social good.

My work as a global HR and OD leader has been instrumental in developing organizational cultures that emphasize the human element at work. By devising strategies for organizations, I have worked with executive leadership teams to kindle environments where respect for the individual is paramount, promoting inclusive practices that acknowledge the unique contributions of every employee. In efforts to nurture a community culture, my method has centered on creating strong, supportive networks within organizations. Through the encouragement of collaboration and open communication, the leadership teams I have worked with enabled a sense of belonging among employees, thereby enhancing teamwork and fueling cooperative success. Another pillar of my work, as evident in *Integrity by Design: Working and Living Authentically*, has been promoting authentic and ethical leadership.[8] By exemplifying integrity and transparency in decision-making, I aim to assist you in establishing leadership standards that uphold trust and accountability.

The Relevance of Humanistic Management Today

People-centered management is more relevant than ever in today's changing workplace. Shifts in work dynamics, driven by technological advancements and the global move towards remote and hybrid work models, have brought the significance of focusing on the human element within the organizational framework to the forefront. One compelling reason for its relevance is the direct correlation between employee engagement and productivity.

A study by Towers Watson underscores this point, revealing that organizations with high employee engagement report a 22% increase in productivity.[9] This data crystallizes the importance of people-centered practices in upholding environments where employees feel valued and motivated, directly linking employee engagement to enhanced customer retention.

Leaders, as the architects of organizational culture, play a fundamental role in nourishing a people-centered environment. Research by the Society for Human Resource Management (SHRM) reveals that a culture of respect and dignity, when championed by leaders, leads to higher levels of job satisfaction and lower turnover rates.[10] By acknowledging everyone's unique contributions, leaders can create a workplace environment that promotes inclusivity and appreciation, thereby contributing to improved performance.

A statistic from Deloitte's 2020 Global Human Capital Trends report emphasizes the growing relevance of people-centered management.[11] The report reveals that 93% of respondents agreed or strongly agreed that a sense of belonging drives organizational performance. This statistic highlights the critical importance of nurturing an inclusive workplace culture where every employee feels valued and connected, a central tenet of people-centered management.

The importance of corporate social responsibility (CSR) and ethical business practices has gained prominence, influencing employee perceptions and loyalty. Employees are more likely to commit to organizations that demonstrate a genuine commitment to social responsibility, including ethical labor practices, environmental sustainability, and community involvement. The Edelman Trust Barometer supports this, indicating that companies perceived as socially responsible command higher trust from their employees, which, in turn, supports a stronger sense of community and organizational loyalty.[12] Therefore, people-centered management not only abets a positive internal work culture but also aligns with broader social values, making it highly relevant in any business ecosystem.

By prioritizing these core principles, organizations can unlock higher levels of innovation and productivity. This demonstrates the significant impact of people-centered management on individual and organizational success, positioning it as a competitive advantage.

Humanistic management and people-centered performance are intrinsically linked, with the former serving as the philosophical foundation for the latter's application in the workplace. Humanistic management celebrates an organizational culture that values each employee's contribution and potential by prioritizing individuals' well-being, development, and fulfillment. This approach naturally leads to people-centered performance, where the focus shifts from narrow productivity metrics to a wider view of success, encompassing employee satisfaction, engagement, and growth. The relationship between humanistic management and people-centered performance underscores a contemporary understanding of organizational excellence, recognizing that truly effective performance is inextricably linked to human capabilities and spirit at its core.

The evolution of this work can also be contextualized within the broader economic shifts that have occurred over the past century. We moved from production-based economies to service-oriented businesses and, most recently, to information and digital economies, particularly in the developed world. This transformation has necessitated a fundamental reevaluation of management practices as the nature of work itself has changed. In the early industrial era, management theories centered mainly on efficiency, standardization, and optimizing labor for production. However, as service industries began to dominate, the focus shifted towards customer satisfaction, employee empowerment, and quality. The information and digital age further accelerated these trends, emphasizing innovation, knowledge work, and digital competencies. These economic transitions have underscored the need for a more nuanced management approach that considers the human elements of creativity, collaboration, and intelligence. As organizations navigate these shifts, the principles of people-centered performance have become increasingly vital, reflecting the growing recognition of the importance of human capital in driving sustainable success.

Historical Foundations and Key Pioneers

The development of the method presented in this book has been deeply influenced by the pioneering work of key figures in psychology and organizational theory, who have highlighted the importance of human values, ethical leadership, and the nurturing of organizational culture. Among these, Abraham Maslow, Carl Rogers, and Mary Parker Follett stand out for their contributions that have significantly shaped how managers and organizations approach cultivating environments that promote personal growth, community, and mutual respect. These are the lessons I learned in graduate school. While I will develop these ideas further in Chapter 7, it seems worthwhile to highlight the pioneers that shaped the approaches presented in *The People Dividend.*

Abraham Maslow's hierarchy of needs provided a profound understanding of employee motivation. It emphasizes that fulfilling employees' higher-level psychological and self-fulfillment needs can lead to more motivated, productive, and satisfied workers. This insight has become a cornerstone in developing people-centered management practices, which focus on creating conditions that allow employees to achieve their full potential.

Carl Rogers, known for his person-centered approach to

psychology, emphasized the power of empathy, active listening, and unconditional positive regard in developing an environment where individuals feel valued and understood. His work has inspired management practices that prioritize genuine connections, open communication, and a supportive atmosphere, enabling employees to thrive personally and professionally.

With her forward-thinking views on management and leadership, Mary Parker Follett advocated for power-sharing through "power-with" rather than "power-over" relationships and the importance of cooperation, negotiation, and integration in the workplace. Her ideas laid the groundwork for collaborative, inclusive management practices that value the voice and contribution of every team member, reinforcing the essence of humanistic management.

These pioneering thought leaders have contributed to a shift away from traditional, hierarchical management models toward more people-focused methods. Their work underlines the transition toward a human-centered paradigm in organization development, highlighting the ongoing evolution from purely mechanical organizational structures to genuinely valuing and nurturing talent.

My people-centered performance model also draws significant inspiration from the contributions of Edie and Charlie Seashore, Warren Bennis, Doug McGregor, Dick Beckhard, and Peter Block, luminaries in the field of OD and the human potential movement. These thought leaders have collectively emphasized the importance of understanding and leveraging human dynamics, potential, and motivation within organizational contexts. From McGregor's Theory X and Theory Y, which juxtapose different views of employee motivation, to Block's focus on stewardship and empowerment, and Bennis's distinction between managing and leading, each has contributed to a complementary framework that values the individual at the heart of organizational processes. Beckhard's strategic insights into organizational change and the Seashores' exploration of group dynamics and interpersonal relationships further enrich this model, embedding principles of transparency, trust, and respect. Together, their pioneering work provides a robust foundation for my system, underscoring the belief that unlocking human potential is key to achieving superior organizational performance.

The historical trajectory of OD reflects a continuous effort to balance operational efficiency with the human needs of workers, integrating principles from psychology, sociology, and systems theory to view the organization in relation to its environment. The contributions of those cited have been essential in this respect, providing important concepts that inform current management practices and guiding a future where businesses succeed by optimizing processes and growing cultures that deeply value the human aspects of work. Through such a lens, the relevance of humanistic values, authentic leadership, integrity, and cultures that promote personal and collective growth becomes increasingly apparent, defining a path for organizations to thrive in an era characterized by change and complexity.

Humanistic Management in Action: Case Examples

Applying people-centered management principles in various organizations worldwide exemplifies the tangible benefits of centering humanistic values in business practices. The following three examples vividly demonstrate how people-centered leadership can significantly improve that which is important to organizational stakeholders.

Examples of Organizations that Embody Humanistic Values

REI (Recreational Equipment, Inc.) is celebrated for its dedication to environmental stewardship and employee well-being. It offers flexible schedules, generous paid time off, and sabbaticals to promote work-life balance. Employees enjoy perks like gear discounts and the "Yay Day" program, which encourages outdoor adventures and conservation efforts. With a focus on diversity and professional growth, REI fosters a supportive culture that aligns employee satisfaction with its mission of promoting outdoor activities and environmental responsibility.[13]

SAS Institute has consistently been recognized for its outstanding workplace culture, high levels of trust, autonomy, and employee benefits. Their approach to management highlights the importance of valuing employees as individuals, which drives innovation and loyalty. This commitment to a people-centered approach enhances employee morale and significantly contributes to the company's overall success and reputation.[14]

Semco Partners, under Ricardo Semler's guidance, has achieved global recognition for its novel methods in management. The company exemplifies the principles of participative management and workplace democracy, offering employees exceptional levels of freedom in determining their work schedules, roles, and involvement in decision-making processes. This culture of autonomy has enhanced employee satisfaction and furthered an environment of improvement and collective responsibility.[15]

Embarking on the path to human-centered management requires an enduring commitment to cultivating a culture that places the well-being, development, and empowerment of every team member at its core. This journey is commanded by a leadership team that embodies empathy, transparency, and open communication, setting a tone that values individual contributions while endowing a collective sense of purpose. By ingraining these principles into the organization's core values, leaders can instill and nurture an environment where employees feel genuinely valued.

To actualize this vision, leaders can implement policies and practices that reflect a sincere interest in employee well-being, such as flexible working arrangements, comprehensive wellness programs, and meaningful learning and development opportunities. As I have consistently learned and practiced, encouraging employee participation in decision-making empowers individuals and enhances performance. Companies can create more engaged workforces by treating employees as whole persons and respecting their lives outside of work. This pathway benefits employees and contributes to the organization's success, proving that putting people first is a strategic choice.

From an Employee Perspective

From the perspective of employees, the workplace presents both opportunities and challenges. Employees today seek more than just a paycheck from their jobs; they seek meaningful work that contributes to their personal and professional growth. For instance, the trend toward remote work has provided employees with unprecedented flexibility, allowing them to balance their personal and professional lives more effectively. However, this shift also requires individuals to possess strong self-management and communication skills as the lines between work and home become increasingly blurred.

Another critical aspect from an employee standpoint is the demand for learning and development. With the pace of technological innovation, skills that were relevant yesterday may become obsolete tomorrow. Employees are, therefore, looking for organizations that invest in their learning and development, providing opportunities for upskilling and reskilling. For example, Google's "Grow with Google" program offers training and professional certificates that help people grow their skills, careers, or businesses, showing how companies can play an essential role in employee development.

Workplace diversity, equity, inclusion, and belonging (DEIB) programs are also paramount from an employee's perspective. In the global business environment, employees seek a workplace where diversity is celebrated and everyone has equitable opportunities to succeed. Salesforce's commitment to DEIB, which includes comprehensive annual equality updates and action plans, is a strong example of how organizations can create an inclusive culture. Such initiatives embed a sense of belonging and drive innovation by bringing diverse perspectives to the table.

The role of feedback and recognition in enhancing the employee experience cannot be overstated. Employees thrive in environments where their contributions are recognized and their voices are heard. Adobe's "Check-In" performance management system, which focuses on regular, timely feedback rather than annual reviews, illustrates how companies can encourage cultures of improvement and recognition.[16]

Leadership greatly impacts employee motivation and engagement. It's often noted that managers and leaders are frequently discussed at family dinner tables. Leaders who demonstrate people-centered behaviors cultivate loyalty and trust among their teams. An example of such leadership is Alex Gorsky, former CEO of Johnson & Johnson.[17] His dedication to ethical practices, employee well-being, and innovative healthcare solutions has significantly contributed to the company's robust culture and sustained success.

Sustainability and corporate social responsibility (CSR) are increasingly becoming factors employees consider when choosing where to work. Employees want to be part of organizations that are committed to making a positive impact on society and the environment. Patagonia's dedication to environmental causes, for instance, enhances its brand reputation and attracts employees who share similar values.

The integration of technology in the workplace is viewed as both positive and negative by employees. While digital tools can enhance productivity and collaboration, there is growing concern about digital overload and the loss of human interaction. Employees increasingly admire organizations that find a balance between using technology and maintaining human connections, such as Slack's efforts to improve communication while promoting work-life balance.

From the viewpoint of employees, an ideal workplace caters to a wide range of their needs, ensuring that they have the opportunity to flourish in both their professional and personal lives. By prioritizing these considerations, organizations are likely to successfully attract, retain, and develop the most talented individuals.

Enhancing Workplace Performance with People-Centered Practices

As described earlier, the correlation between people-centered management and productivity is intuitive and empirically supported. This relationship becomes clearer when examining the intrinsic motivation employees experience when they feel integral to their organization's goals. Such environments elevate productivity and contribute to a culture of sustained improvement.

In the tech industry, the repercussions of poor management and leadership practices are stark. These practices have been directly linked to significant adverse outcomes, including marked decreases in productivity. The tech sector's relentless pursuit of productivity often results in toxic work environments that hinder output and innovation.[18] Furthermore, the tech industry's quest for peak productivity is ironic in that it can sometimes lead to counterproductive work cultures.[19] These examples underscore the critical need for people-centered management to avoid such detrimental effects, particularly in fields where the pace of change and innovation is relentless.

Under the umbrella of people-centered management, creativity thrives. A culture that encourages risk-taking, values diverse perspectives, and treats failures as learning opportunities becomes a proving ground for success. When employees are liberated from the fear of judgment or repercussions for thinking outside the box, they are more likely to propose groundbreaking ideas that propel an organization forward. This highlights the central role of people-centered management in advancing innovation, undeniably crucial for organizational growth.

For example, Google, known for its innovative edge and dominance in the tech industry, famously encourages its employees to spend 20% of their work time on personal projects that interest them.[20] This policy, rooted in people-centered management, has created some of Google's most successful products, such as Gmail and AdSense. By treating failures as learning opportunities, Google has cultivated an environment where creativity flourishes. Employees feel able to propose groundbreaking ideas without fear of judgment or repercussion, moving the company forward and setting it apart from competitors. This path underlines the importance of creating and maintaining a supportive work culture and showcases how employee freedom can lead to significant innovations. This creative liberty sets a company apart from its competitors.

The immediate benefit of people-centered management is that it enhances employee engagement, which leads to better customer outcomes. Companies can significantly elevate engagement levels by considering employees as their most valuable asset. Engaged employees are not just more loyal and less likely to leave; they also become advocates for their company, attracting like-minded talent and boosting a positive public image. This underscores the direct correlation between people-centered management and customer growth and retention.

To cultivate a people-centered culture, leaders must commit to an overarching shift that prioritizes employees' needs and experiences. This involves regular and open communication, genuine efforts to understand and accommodate diverse employee needs, and a commitment to ongoing improvement. Tangible actions that demonstrate a company's devotion to its people include inspiring collaboration and teamwork, recognizing and rewarding contributions, and promoting from within. The pathway to success begins with leadership's willingness to view success through the lens of their people's well-being and fulfillment.

Tools and Strategies for Implementing People-Centered Management

Implementing people-centered management requires a shift in both mindset and practice. Managers play a crucial role in this transformation, serving as models for the values and behaviors that define a human-centered workplace. Here are some practical tips and strategies for embedding humanistic values into an organizational culture:

1. **Lead by example:** Demonstrate empathy, transparency, and respect in every interaction. Leaders should embody the humanistic values they wish to see throughout the organization.

2. **Foster open communication:** Encourage a culture where feedback is welcomed and valued. Implement regular check-ins and open forums where employees feel safe to express their thoughts and ideas.

3. **Invest in development:** Support employees' personal and professional growth through training programs, mentorship opportunities, and career development plans. Show genuine interest in their aspirations and well-being.

4. **Recognize and reward:** Acknowledge individual and team achievements publicly and regularly. Use recognition to reinforce behaviors that align with the organization's values, boosting morale and encouraging continued excellence.

5. **Promote well-being:** Implement flexible working

hours, remote work options, and policies that support a healthy blend between work and personal life. Recognizing the importance of mental health and well-being contributes to a productive workforce.

By integrating these strategies, organizations can foster a human-centered culture that enhances productivity and creativity and ensures employee satisfaction and well-being. A workplace prioritizing empathy, open communication, and personal growth creates a more motivated and loyal workforce. Recognizing achievements, supporting work-life balance, and encouraging diversity and inclusivity lead to a more innovative and resilient organization. Ultimately, people-centered management transforms the workplace into a thriving environment where both employees and the organization can flourish.

Conclusion

The shift towards people-centered management underscores a significant evolution in organizational philosophy, emphasizing success through genuine engagement and employee welfare. The unceasing importance of people-centered management for the future of work is critical to success. As the workforce continues evolving amid technological advancements and shifting expectations, the need for workplaces to prioritize human values over efficiency metrics becomes increasingly crucial. The future of work demands a paradigm where employee well-being is a precursor to economic success. Adopting humanistic management practices creates a strategic advantage.

The shift towards people-centered management will mark a crucial evolution in how organizations conceptualize employee engagement. The approaches I presented in this chapter provide an important framework for cultivating a workplace that prioritizes people. By redefining what it means to be successful, these strategies emphasize the importance of including metrics (more on this in Chapter Three) of employee engagement and well-being alongside traditional financial indicators. This dual focus ensures a more rounded way of assessing organizational health and underscores the integral role employees play in achieving business goals. Encouraging participatory decision-making further empowers employees, giving them a voice in shaping the direction and policies of the organization, which in turn instills a deep sense of ownership and commitment.

Adopting a people-centered strategy in management and organization development strategies is beneficial and essential in creating an extraordinary workplace. This change represents a broader move towards more empathetic and humane business practices, setting a new standard for excellence in the corporate world. Organizations that commit to these principles are likely to see financial success and a more engaged workforce.

Reflection Questions for Chapter One

- How can leaders incorporate empathy into their management practices?

- What are the benefits of a workplace that prioritizes employee well-being?

- How can open communication impact organizational culture?

- In what ways can recognition of achievements motivate employees?

- How does a human-centered workplace contribute to the overall performance of an organization?

Chapter 2

Respect and Dignity: Building a Culture of Mutual Regard

How do you respond when respect and dignity are at stake in your workplace?

As a human resources (HR) leader at a large biopharmaceutical company, I once had to navigate a difficult situation involving Martin, the head of our research and development team. During one of the scientific progress reviews, Linda, a gifted researcher, was presenting her findings to a room full of colleagues when Martin sharply criticized her work and questioned her competence, leaving her feeling embarrassed and demoralized in front of everyone. Linda didn't let this slide; she showed remarkable bravery by coming to me and reporting the incident. This sparked an investigation into Martin's behavior and underscored the importance of fostering respect and professionalism within our team. It was pivotal in reinforcing our commitment to a supportive and respectful workplace culture.

Are you curious about what happened next?

The confrontation between Martin and Linda could have been a moment that eroded trust and confidence within the team. However, it also presented an opportunity for growth and reaffirmation of core values. By addressing issues head-on rather than sweeping them under the rug, we can set a precedent that upholds the inherent worth of every team member, spotlighting the non-negotiable importance of treating each other with dignity and respect. This scenario underscores the role of HR and organizational leaders in promoting an environment that paves the way for constructive dialogue and mutual understanding.

The importance of respect and dignity in the workplace is undeniable. These foundational elements elevate employee engagement, boost efficiency, and are essential for progress. More than just simple politeness, respect encompasses acknowledging every individual's intrinsic value, celebrating diverse backgrounds, and creating a venue where every voice can be heard. In this chapter, we explore the critical importance of respect and dignity in leadership, using Linda's experience as our starting point. The incident between Martin and Linda was not merely an interpersonal conflict; it reflected deeper issues regarding how individuals are treated within an organizational context. Such incidents challenge us to reconsider how principles of dignity and respect are upheld and integrated into organizational life. We will uncover the substantial effects of a respectful culture on employee well-being and productivity, highlighting examples of transformations through respect and dignity. By exploring these stories, it will become evident that emphasizing respect and dignity benefits not only the individuals within an organization but also plays an essential role in its enduring prosperity. Respect and dignity are foundational to reaping the rewards of the people dividend.

Understanding Respect and Dignity in the Workplace

The civil rights activist, poet, and Presidential Medal of Freedom award winner Maya Angelou famously said, "I've learned that people will forget what you said, people will forget what you did, but people will never forget how you made them feel." This sentiment lies at the heart of fostering a culture centered on respect and dignity. It encompasses recognizing the inherent value of each person, ensuring equitable treatment, and promoting an atmosphere of mutual understanding and appreciation. In this section, we will define and unravel the nuances of respect and dignity, exploring their significance and profound influence on workplace dynamics. Through this examination, I aim to provide actionable insights and strategies to embed these crucial values deeply within the workplace cultures.

At its core, dignity refers to the essential worth and value everyone possesses simply by being human. It's an internal state of being that demands recognition and acknowledgment, irrespective of one's status, achievements, or contributions. This intrinsic worth means everyone deserves to be treated with kindness, fairness, and consideration, thereby creating an environment where individuals feel important. For example, a manager demonstrates the value of dignity by actively listening to each team member's opinions and concerns during meetings.

On the other hand, respect often operates as the outward expression of acknowledging someone's dignity. It involves recognizing and appreciating each person's unique qualities, abilities, and perspectives. Respect in the workplace manifests through actions and words that honor an individual's contributions and value their presence. For example, a manager demonstrates respect by seeking employee's ideas before making significant decisions.

The relationship between dignity and respect in an organizational context is symbiotic. Recognizing the inherent dignity of all employees lays the foundation for a culture of respect. When people feel their dignity is acknowledged, they are more likely to engage respectfully with others, encouraging collaboration and belonging. This understanding of the relationship between dignity and respect underscores the importance of each individual's role in introjecting these values and their impact on workplace dynamics and organizational success. Conversely, a lack of respect can undermine dignity, leading to disengagement, dissatisfaction, and conflict.

Thus, maintaining a balance where dignity is upheld and respect is consistently demonstrated becomes essential to success. While dignity denotes an individual's inherent value, respect acknowledges and affirms that value within the organizational framework. Together, they form the bedrock of a healthy, productive workplace environment, driving mutual understanding, cooperation, and achievement. Organizations prioritizing these principles enhance their operational effectiveness and contribute to a more equitable and fulfilling work experience for every member.

The practical implementation of respect and dignity in the workplace extends beyond policy manuals or corporate statements—it is actualized in the daily interactions and decisions that define a company's culture. It involves leaders modeling these values through transparent communication, empathy, and accountability in their leadership styles. Equally, it requires systems that unequivocally support diversity, equity, and inclusion, ensuring every team member, regardless of their background or role, has access to the same opportunities and is judged by their contributions and performance. This empowering approach not only endows a more equitable environment but also enriches the workplace with various perspectives, leading to advanced solutions and a competitive edge. By committing to these principles, organizations can transform respect and dignity from abstract ideals into the mainstays of their corporate identity, setting a new standard for accomplishment.

The Evolution of Workplace Culture towards Inclusivity

Throughout history, workplace environments have often prioritized hierarchy and authority, sometimes at the expense of fostering a dignified and respectful atmosphere. However, in recent years, there has been a significant shift towards recognizing and valuing the diverse backgrounds of all employees. This change is not just a trend but a strategic move driven by an increased awareness of the benefits of a culture where everyone's contributions are appreciated and where all can flourish. Workplaces that emphasize respect and dignity tend to be more cohesive and creative, promoting the open sharing of ideas and teamwork, which leads to improved employee well-being and business success.

Genentech, a leader in the biotechnology industry, is renowned for its groundbreaking contributions to healthcare and its progressive workplace culture that values inclusivity and respect.[21] This commitment to dignity and respect is a strategic and principled choice, reflecting broader shifts in global business expectations. When I hired Cori Davis into Genentech and onto my organization development (OD) team, it was clear she would play a pivotal role in driving these values forward. Companies at the forefront of this transition, such as Genentech, have reported improved employee happiness and morale, enhanced reputations, remarkable patient outcomes, and stronger long-term financial results. Therefore, implementing respect and dignity at work is essential for building a competitive and sustainable business.

Adapting to this changing workplace culture requires that organizations take a proactive stance on inclusivity. It involves regularly reviewing and adjusting policies, procedures, and behaviors to ensure they reflect values of respect and dignity. This change also includes understanding the diverse needs and wants of the workforce, leading to fairer and more equitable working conditions. For example, many organizations are now developing policies regarding gender construction and identity.

Beyond its efforts to cultivate diversity and support, Genentech has taken significant steps to address the well-being of its employees, notably through its recent focus on mental health initiatives and comprehensive menopause benefits. In response to the increasing recognition of the crucial role of mental health in overall well-being, Genentech has introduced a range of support services and resources. These initiatives include access to counseling services, mental health days, and programs to reduce stigma and promote open conversations about mental health. Additionally, Genentech has pioneered offering extensive menopause benefits, recognizing an often-overlooked area of women's health. This includes providing access to specialized healthcare, educational resources, and workplace accommodations, ensuring employees going through menopause receive the support and understanding they need.

These specific initiatives demonstrate Genentech's commitment to creating a workplace that respects and responds to its employees' diverse health and wellness needs. In recent interviews, Cori Davis, chief people officer at Genentech, emphasized the importance of menopause benefits in upholding a sense of belonging and inclusion among employees.[22] She believes these benefits are crucial for employee retention and overall workplace wellness. These enhancements to employee benefits reflect Genentech's deep commitment to respecting and dignifying its staff.

By directly addressing mental health and menopause,

Genentech sets a precedent for proactive and compassionate workplace policies. These measures affirm the company's dedication to its employees' health and happiness and contribute to a culture of innovation. Genentech demonstrates how prioritizing employees' physical and mental health is integral to building a competitive, sustainable, and highly respectful workplace.

The strides taken by organizations like Genentech in cultivating a respectful workplace culture contribute directly to unlocking the full potential of their talent. These efforts enhance employee engagement and create a more inclusive environment where innovation can thrive. By prioritizing respect and dignity, companies improve their internal dynamics and set an example for others in the industry to follow.

Dignity and Respect at Work

At its core, respect in the workplace manifests as a recognition of each individual's worth and contributions, regardless of position or background. It means actively listening to others' ideas, providing constructive feedback, and showing appreciation for their efforts. Dignity, on the other hand, involves treating everyone with fairness and integrity, thereby ensuring that the workplace becomes a space where everyone feels safe, valued, and empowered to express themselves. Both respect and dignity are essential for growing a positive organizational culture that encourages collaboration and teamwork.

Defining respect and dignity begins with understanding

their practical implications in daily workplace interactions. For instance, respect is demonstrated through actions like honoring agreements, respecting personal boundaries, and valuing others' time and efforts by being punctual and prepared for meetings. Dignity is similarly expressed by adopting policies that support work-life balance, ensuring equitable treatment for all employees, and creating avenues for every voice to be heard and acknowledged. These values must be communicated and exemplified at all levels of an organization, from the C-suite to the frontline.

Organizations must adopt a multi-layered approach to embed respect and dignity effectively. This includes developing and enforcing clear policies that address and prevent harassment and discrimination, creating channels for employees to report grievances without fear of retribution, and investing in development programs that educate employees on the importance of respect and dignity in developing an inclusive workplace. Leaders play a crucial role in this process; they must lead by example, demonstrating respect and dignity in their interactions and decision-making and setting the tone for the behavior expected throughout the organization.

When consulting on performance management improvement with the chief HR officer at Gap, I was always impressed by the company's robust zero-tolerance policy regarding child labor. Gap enforces strict supplier standards, conducts unannounced audits, and implements remediation programs to ensure compliance and uphold ethical sourcing practices. This commitment is a powerful demonstration of dignity for all, ensuring that every worker, regardless of employer, is treated with respect and dignity.

Failing to effectively articulate and integrate the values of respect and dignity within the workplace can have far-reaching consequences for individuals and the organization. Without these guiding principles, workplaces can become breeding grounds for toxic behaviors and attitudes, such as bullying, harassment, and discrimination. This undermines employees' sense of safety and value, leading to increased stress, lower job satisfaction, and higher turnover rates. On an organizational level, the absence of respect and dignity can tarnish a company's reputation, hinder its ability to attract and retain top talent, and result in financial losses due to legal actions and decreased productivity. It underscores the importance of asserting these values not only in policy documents but also in living them out through every action and decision, thereby safeguarding the well-being of the workforce and the integrity of the organization.

Research Findings on Respect in the Workplace

A wealth of empirical research on dignity and respect in the workplace highlights their critical importance. Scholars from various disciplines have contributed to our understanding of workplace dignity, exploring its nuances beyond its basic premises. Scholars such as Amy Edmondson, Jeffrey Pfeffer, Teresa Amabile, James G. March, and Will Kymlicka made substantial contributions to this field. Studies have distinguished between inherent dignity, which every person possesses simply by being human, and earned dignity, based on an individual's achievements or behavior within a professional setting. This multidimensional view emphasizes that while inherent dignity is universal and non-negotiable, earned dignity can vary and plays a significant role in workplace dynamics and relationships.

Further research has focused on developing tools like the Workplace Dignity Scale to measure the presence and impact of dignity.[23] Findings from these studies underscore the incremental validity of dignity in explaining employee well-being and engagement beyond what is accounted for by meaningful work alone. Such insights suggest that advancing workplace dignity involves more than just promoting respect; it requires creating conditions where employees feel genuinely valued and recognized. This consists of addressing and remediating instances of disrespect or indignity and proactively cultivating an environment that supports dignity. Through this body of research, it becomes clear that dignity in the workplace is a complex phenomenon deeply intertwined with concepts of respect, meaningful work, and organizational culture, playing a crucial role in shaping employees' experiences and organizational outcomes.

Recent research underlines the critical impact of respect on employee engagement and loyalty. A study by the Society for Human Resource Management (SHRM) found that employees who rated their organizations highly on respect were five times more likely to report high levels of engagement than those in less respectful environments.[24] This engagement translates into deeper loyalty and a more substantial commitment, reducing turnover rates significantly. A *Harvard Business Review* article by

Christine Porath, "Half of Employees Don't Feel Respected by Their Bosses," reported that a study of nearly 20,000 employees worldwide found that respect is crucial for garnering employee commitment and engagement.[25]

Furthermore, the link between respectful work environments and organizational performance is clear. Research by the Gallup Organization shows a direct correlation between employee engagement, spurred by respect, and higher productivity, profitability, and customer ratings.[26] Companies with cultures characterized by high levels of respect reported earnings per share growth at more than four times the rate of competitors with less respectful cultures.

Diversity also plays a significant role in the positive outcomes associated with respect. McKinsey & Company's research reaffirms that diverse and inclusive workplaces, where respect is a given, outperform industry norms on profitability.[27] Their latest report indicates that companies in the top quartile for gender diversity on their executive teams were 25% more likely to have above average profitability than companies in the fourth quartile. This margin is even more significant for ethnic and cultural diversity, with a 36% likelihood of outperformance on profitability for the most diverse companies.[28]

However, instilling a culture of respect transcends hiring practices and diversity metrics. It involves creating an environment where every employee, regardless of background or seniority level, feels valued, heard, and integral to the organization. This requires consistent effort and genuine commitment from leadership alongside structured programs and initiatives designed to champion respect at all levels.

Investments in respect and inclusion training, establishing transparent and responsive feedback mechanisms, and upholding a zero-tolerance policy for disrespect and discrimination are foundational. Such strategies reinforce the core values of respect and dignity and chart a path toward sustained organizational success, marked by innovative outcomes, superior performance, and a competitive edge.

The empirical evidence underscores the significant payoff of creating an environment where every employee feels respected. To make this a reality, leadership must actively model the values of dignity and respect, ensuring that these principles are embedded in every level of the organization, from recruitment to retirement. By making dignity and respect central to culture, you not only enhance employee engagement but unlock a level of loyalty, creativity, and productivity that can propel your company to new heights. This requires a commitment to ongoing learning, listening, and adaptability, ensuring that respect and dignity evolve in line with your organization's growth and the diverse needs of your workforce.

Furthermore, the drive for a respectful workplace should inspire progressive practices and policies recognizing each employee's unique contributions. Initiatives like structured mentorship programs, recognition systems that celebrate big and small achievements, and open forums for feedback and dialogue can be powerful tools for reinforcing a culture of respect.

Leaders can inspire a ripple effect throughout their organizations, creating an environment where respect fuels performance and diversity and inclusion become the engines of success. By prioritizing respect and dignity, you build a better workplace and set a standard for excellence in your industry, attracting top talent and growing a brand synonymous with integrity and innovation. In doing so, HR and business leaders can achieve remarkable organizational outcomes and contribute to shaping a more inclusive and respectful society.

The Business Case for Fostering Respect

According to Kristie Rogers in *Do Your Employees Feel Respected?*, employees who feel respected are more engaged, committed, and satisfied.[29] These findings underscore that respect directly influences an organization's performance metrics. Take REI (Recreational Equipment, Inc.), mentioned previously, which has cultivated a strong culture of environmental stewards and well-being, leading to notable improvements in employee satisfaction and brand loyalty.

Respectful workplaces are more likely to attract and retain top talent, enhancing their competitive edge. Charles Handy, professor of Organizational Behavior at London Business School, Herminia Ibarra, highlights that respect is an essential feedback mechanism that fosters growth and innovation.[30] When employees feel respected, they are more motivated to contribute to their fullest potential, aiding trust and cooperation. For instance, since its founding in 1978 by Ben Cohen and Jerry Greenfield, Ben & Jerry's has actively promoted a culture of respect by implementing progressive employee policies and community-focused initiatives. This commitment to respect and inclusivity continued even after the company was acquired by Unilever in 2000. Even today, nearly fifty years later, Ben & Jerry's continues to see remarkable outcomes in employee morale and productivity, reinforcing that respect is indispensable to a successful business strategy.[31]

How Respect Drives Employee Satisfaction and Productivity

Workplace respect is a powerful catalyst for employee satisfaction and productivity. When team members feel valued and respected, they experience a greater sense of belonging and connection with their work. This psychological safety encourages people to take calculated risks, share novel ideas, and contribute more willingly to team goals. Research consistently shows a direct correlation between enhanced productivity and respectful environments. Employees in such environments are more likely to extend their discretionary efforts to the company's performance objectives.

Beyond individual satisfaction and productivity, respect within the workplace significantly impacts an organization's ability to innovate and maintain a competitive edge. In an environment where diverse perspectives are valued and encouraged, there is a natural increase in the variety and quality of ideas being generated. This diversity of thought leads to advanced problem-solving methods and processes, crucial for organizations seeking to adapt and thrive in today's environment. Respectful workplaces attract talent from various backgrounds, experiences, and cultures, enriching the organization's intellectual pool and enhancing its creative and adaptive powers. By nurturing a culture of respect, businesses position themselves as leaders.

Furthermore, the ripple effects of a culture of respect extend to customer interactions and the broader community. Employees who feel respected and valued are more likely to convey these positive attitudes in their engagement with customers, leading to improved customer loyalty. This enhanced customer experience becomes a powerful brand differentiator. Additionally, businesses that demonstrate a commitment to respect and dignity within their workplace are often viewed more favorably by the public. This positive public perception can increase opportunities for business partnerships, collaborations, and growth within the community. Instilling respect and dignity in the workplace is not just an internal policy but a choice that shapes every facet of the organization's public image.

The Link Between Respect, Innovation, and Competitive Advantage

Cultivating respect in the workplace is substantially linked to innovation, as diversity of thought is a valuable resource for driving creativity and problem-solving. When employees feel respected, they are more inclined to present new ideas and challenge existing notions, leading to breakthroughs that can significantly enhance competitive advantage.

Respect also plays a crucial role in talent attraction and retention. Organizations known for their respectful and inclusive cultures attract a wider talent pool, including top performers who seek environments where they can thrive. A strong reputation for respect and inclusivity enhances an organization's employer brand, making it more appealing to prospective employees. Furthermore, lower turnover rates reduce the high costs of recruiting and training new employees.

Investing in learning and development programs focused on building a culture of respect is essential. These programs should define what respect means in the workplace and equip employees with the skills to communicate respectfully, provide constructive feedback, and manage conflicts positively. By institutionalizing respect through policy, practice, and education, organizations can ensure that respect becomes an integral part of their culture.

The business case for fostering respect within the workplace is compelling. It leads to improved employee satisfaction and productivity, enhanced innovation, and a competitive edge in talent attraction and retention. Ultimately, respect is a strategic advantage, crucial for long-term success. In the next section, I offer practical advice for embedding respect into the DNA of workplace culture, ensuring it transitions from an aspirational value to a lived experience.

Strategies for Cultivating a Respectful Workplace

Creating a workplace culture of respect and dignity is essential for maintaining a positive work environment. While policies and procedures provide a framework for behavior, the attitudes and actions of individuals at every level of an organization genuinely shape the culture. Leadership plays a critical role, as do the policies and practices that support respect and dignity. In addition, it's essential to address and correct disrespectful behaviors. Through these strategies, organizations can develop a workplace that prioritizes respect and dignity, benefiting from the enhanced performance these values support.

Advancing a culture of respect requires consistent effort and commitment from all levels of an organization, especially leadership. Leaders must actively model respectful behaviors in their daily interactions and decision-making processes. They should also recognize and promptly address any disrespect, whether in the form of microaggressions, discrimination, or harassment. This commitment sends a powerful message throughout the organization, reinforcing the importance of respect and its non-negotiable status within the company's values.

Policies and Practices that Support Respect and Dignity

Leadership modeling is pivotal in fostering a respectful organizational culture, but establishing concrete policies and practices is equally vital. Clear anti-discrimination policies, transparent communication channels, and regular diversity, equity, inclusion, and belonging (DEIB) initiatives are necessary. These frameworks ensure that every employee feels a sense of belonging and respect regardless of background or identity.

Feedback mechanisms are crucial for maintaining this culture, providing a way to gauge the effectiveness of ongoing initiatives and identify areas needing improvement. Taking employee feedback seriously and acting upon it showcases a genuine commitment to fostering a respectful workplace. Implementing robust, anonymous feedback systems builds trust and openness, encouraging employees to voice concerns or suggestions without fear.

Moreover, clear and fair processes for addressing concerns and conflicts further underline an organization's commitment to respect. Employees need assurance that their feedback will be welcomed and acted upon. Institutionalizing these processes maintains a respectful culture and enhances overall employee satisfaction and productivity. This dedication to respect and openness ultimately strengthens the organization, fostering a positive work environment where innovation and engagement can thrive.

When combined with leadership's authentic modeling of respect and dignity, these measures create a robust foundation for a positive workplace culture. Reflecting on this, how might leaders in your organization reinforce respect and dignity in their teams, and what ripple effects could this produce in the broader organizational culture?

Leadership's Role in Modeling and Promoting Respect

The influence of leadership in supporting a workplace that prioritizes respect and dignity is paramount. Leaders shape organizational culture through actions and communication, requiring them to embody respect and dignity in every interaction and decision. By living these values, leaders establish behavior standards integral to the company's atmosphere.

Consider an executive from a leading software development firm who significantly impacted how respect and dignity are perceived within her organization. She introduced "Open Door Days," allowing employees to discuss ideas, issues, or feedback with her directly. This policy underscores her respect for all team members' contributions and promotes an environment of acknowledgment and open dialogue. This initiative has nurtured a culture of respect and open communication, ensuring employees feel integral to the company's operations.

Additionally, she shared her experiences with professional setbacks during all-hands meetings, humanizing the leadership role and demonstrating that vulnerability is a strength. This transparency helps break down barriers between management and employees, promoting a culture of openness, honesty, and mutual support. Her commitment to transparency has led to higher levels of employee engagement, showing the positive impact that respectful leadership can have on an organization's success.

The significance of leadership in championing dignity in the workplace is clear. The actions of the software development firm's executive illustrate how a commitment from leadership can catalyze positive organizational behaviors. By fostering open communication, leaders set an admirable standard reflecting core values of respect and dignity, initiating a shift towards greater engagement and innovation. How might leaders in your organization integrate these values, and what impact could this leadership style have on team cohesion and driving innovation?

Addressing and Correcting Disrespectful Behaviors

Despite the foundational role of leadership modeling and the establishment of comprehensive policies, challenges in maintaining a culture of respect and dignity can still surface. Instances of disrespectful behavior may emerge, underscoring the need for organizations to be equipped with effective mechanisms to address such incidents. It's not just about having rules in place; it's about ensuring a transparent, accessible process for reporting behaviors that go against the organization's values. This framework should include straightforward procedures for investigating incidents and applying consistent repercussions to those violating the established standards of respect and dignity. In the workplace, behaviors that undermine respect and dignity can manifest in various forms, illustrating the importance of vigilance and accountability. In reviewing these examples, consider the case of Martin and Linda in the introduction to this chapter.

Disrespect and dignity-reducing behaviors are demonstrated when employees engage in or tolerate bullying, whether through verbal insults, mockery, or rumors about colleagues. Exclusion from meetings or team activities, not based on relevant criteria but personal biases, also severely impacts an individual's sense of belonging and value. Additionally, dismissing or ignoring someone's contributions without consideration or making decisions that affect someone's role without their input directly contravenes principles of respect and dignity. Public reprimands that could have been addressed privately embarrass the individual and erode trust within the team. Whether overt or subtle, each of these behaviors signals a disregard for the fundamental principles of respect and dignity. Swift and decisive action in these situations is non-negotiable. Organizations must reinforce their commitment by responding promptly to reports of disrespectful behavior. This commitment is critical in instilling an environment where employees feel valued. It also serves as a powerful deterrent against future violations, demonstrating that the organization's principles are actionable standards that guide conduct.

Furthermore, an organization's ability to handle such challenges with integrity and transparency can strengthen trust. Employees who see their concerns taken seriously and addressed appropriately are more likely to be loyal and feel engaged with their employer. This trust is critical in a culture that actively discourages disrespect.

Leaders are responsible not just for setting the example but also for enforcing it. How might leaders in your organization ensure that their actions and the systems they implement effectively deter disrespect and uphold the dignity of every team member? What steps can enhance transparency and trust in the processes designed to protect these values?

Implementing and Sustaining a Culture of Respect

Building a workplace that champions respect and dignity is complex, necessitating thoughtful planning and unwavering dedication. Implementing a culture of respect is both a challenge and a necessity to transform abstract values into tangible outcomes. This section provides an overview of the actionable steps and recurring efforts required to build and maintain a culture of respect and dignity. By focusing on strategic initiatives and accountability measures, companies can ensure that values become pillars of their mission, enriching every employee's work life and enhancing the organization's overall performance and reputation.

The goal is to grow an environment where the principles of respect and dignity are integral to the organization's culture. Below are seven essential steps to cultivate such a culture.

Steps for Building Respect and Dignity in Work Environments

1. **Establishing clear expectations:** Clearly define and

communicate the behaviors that demonstrate respect and dignity within the organization. These criteria should be consistently applied across all organizational activities, from recruitment to performance reviews, embedding them into the company's core values.

2. **Comprehensive development:** Implement regular, mandatory development experiences for all employees that cover the specific actions that uphold a culture of respect and dignity. These development experiences establish a shared understanding and lay the groundwork for a respectful workplace.

3. **Empowering employees:** Ensure a safe space for employees to express concerns over disrespectful or undignified behavior without fear of reprisal. Empowerment also means actively involving employees in decision-making processes and acknowledging their contributions, which promotes a sense of belonging and mutual respect.

4. **Creating inclusion:** Create an environment where everyone feels included. Appreciating a broad spectrum of perspectives and backgrounds—including cultural, racial, experiential, and cognitive diversity—will enrich the organizational culture with varied viewpoints and ideas.

5. **Regular feedback and dialogue:** Encourage continuous feedback and open dialogue among all organizational levels. This helps identify and address potential conflicts early on and strengthens a culture of mutual understanding and respect.

6. **Accountability and enforcement:** Maintain a zero-tolerance policy for any breach of respect and dignity, ensuring consistent and equitable enforcement of these

standards. Uniformly applying repercussions underscores the organization's commitment to a respectful and dignified work environment.

7. **Regular Assessment and improvement:** Routinely evaluate the effectiveness of current policies and practices, remaining open to adjustments. Cultivating a respectful and dignified workplace is a dynamic process that benefits from frequent evaluation and adaptation.

By diligently adhering to these steps, organizations can ensure that respect and dignity are active and defining elements of the workplace. Such a commitment will significantly enhance employee performance.

Measuring and Sustaining Respect Over Time

Measuring and sustaining respect over time, particularly without relying heavily on surveys or direct feedback mechanisms, demands inventive and action-oriented strategies. These strategies are not just suggestions but crucial steps for HR and business leaders committed to ensuring that a culture of respect and dignity thrives in their organizations. Here are specific, measurable actions to consider:

1. **Observation of interactions:** Regular, informal observations of day-to-day employee interactions can be insightful. This is a practical and effective way to gauge your organization's respect and dignity levels. Look for signs of positive engagement, such as active listening, collaboration, and inclusive behavior in meetings and common areas. Conversely, note any instances of

65

exclusionary behavior or conflict to identify areas for improvement.

2. **Turnover and retention rates:** Analyze turnover and retention rates focusing on departments or teams with notably high or low figures. This analysis can provide valuable insights into your organization's respect and dignity culture. Departments with lower turnover might indicate healthier respect and dignity levels, while higher turnover could signal areas needing attention. Diving deeper into exit interview data can also provide indirect insights into the respect and dignity culture.

3. **Promotion and advancement opportunities:** Monitor the diversity and equity of promotion and advancement opportunities. A transparent and fair process that promotes individuals from a wide range of backgrounds suggests a respectful recognition of diverse talents and contributions.

4. **Behavioral incident reports:** Track formal and informal reports related to workplace behavior. An increase or decrease in such reports can serve as a barometer for the organization's cultural health regarding respect and dignity. It's essential to note improvements or deteriorations over time and respond accordingly.

5. **Participation in voluntary programs:** Engagement levels in voluntary programs, especially those related to diversity and inclusion initiatives, can also serve as an indirect measure. High participation rates often reflect a respected and valued workforce, encouraging active contributions to the organization's culture.

Ensuring these measures lead to meaningful change requires careful observation and analysis and a commitment to action based on the insights gained. Leaders should be prepared to initiate targeted interventions where necessary, such as revisiting training programs, adjusting policies to close gaps in equity and inclusion, or enhancing conflict resolution processes. Maintaining a culture of respect and dignity is an ongoing process, necessitating agility and responsiveness from leadership. It is critical to translate observations and data into tangible improvements, reinforcing the organization's dedication and commitment to a work environment where every employee is valued and respected.

By focusing on actionable metrics, HR and other business leaders can gain valuable insights into respect and dignity within their organizations. This facilitates a proactive stance towards nurturing a respectful work environment, allowing leaders to tailor interventions and recognize progress beyond traditional feedback methods. It also underscores the ongoing commitment required to embed respect deep into the organizational fabric, ensuring that it remains a living, evolving aspect of the company's culture.

Success Stories and Lessons Learned

The following success stories from diverse organizations highlight several strategies that significantly improved employee morale, productivity, and overall company performance. Additionally, I'll distill key lessons from these experiences to provide valuable insights that can guide other organizations in cultivating a culture of respect and dignity. By examining these examples, you will come to understand the practical applications and benefits of the principles discussed in the previous sections, reinforcing the imperative of building and maintaining a respectful work environment.

Numerous organizations have taken the lead in cultivating workplace environments where respect, dignity, and inclusion are paramount, showcasing original strategies and dedication to these principles. These efforts underscore diversity's immense value to corporate life and a commitment to ensuring every individual within the organization feels genuinely valued, heard, and respected. By implementing comprehensive diversity and inclusion programs, creating supportive employee resource groups, and maintaining an atmosphere where open dialogue is encouraged and celebrated, these companies aim to set a new standard for corporate culture.

However, this journey is full of challenges and obstacles. Even those organizations widely regarded as leaders in workplace respect and inclusion have faced their share of scrutiny and criticism. Issues ranging from balancing company policies with individual rights of expression to managing diverse and sometimes diverging viewpoints highlight the delicate nature of this ongoing work. These critiques serve as a powerful reminder of the steady effort required to cultivate cultures that honor the principles of respect, dignity, and inclusion.

In undertaking this mission, these organizations strive to create more harmonious and productive working environments and reflect a broader commitment to social responsibility and ethical leadership. By navigating this complex terrain and acknowledging achievements and challenges, they contribute significantly to advancing the conversation around what it means to be a workplace that genuinely respects and dignifies every member of its community.

Microsoft is committed to diversity and inclusion through its global initiatives.[32] The company supports ERGs for women, veterans, and people of different cultural backgrounds, providing platforms for employees to connect and advocate for change. Microsoft also promotes diversity through "Unconscious Bias Training" and "Inclusive Hiring" programs to educate employees and develop inclusive workplace skills. Despite facing challenges like employee concerns about diversity, which led to public scrutiny and internal reviews, Microsoft's efforts highlight the complexities of fostering an inclusive culture in tech. Its initiatives show a solid commitment to diversity and the need for ongoing effort and adaptation.

Salesforce is recognized for putting equality at the heart of its business philosophy, actively working towards closing pay gaps, and offering flexible working conditions to honor the diverse needs of its employees.[33] Yet, Salesforce has faced criticism for managing employee activism and dissent, indicating tension between corporate actions and proclaimed values of respect and inclusion.

The World Wildlife Fund (WWF) showcases how non-profits can also excel in creating respectful and inclusive environments.[34] With a mission centered around conservation, WWF extends this ethos to its workplace culture, emphasizing diversity, equity, and inclusion through initiatives like targeted training on cultural competency. This focus ensures that diverse perspectives are not merely accepted but viewed as critical to achieving effective conservation outcomes.

Patagonia distinguishes itself in the retail and outdoor industry by deeply integrating social and environmental responsibility into its corporate identity.[35] The company's support for environmental activism and its emphasis on work-life balance manifests its commitment to an inclusive workplace aligned with its broader mission. Patagonia's efforts underline the importance of creating a cohesive culture that respects the planet and its people.

These organizations illustrate the enduring challenge of building inclusive, respectful workplaces. Despite their successes, they also need help aligning corporate policies with employee beliefs and expectations. This balancing act underscores that cultivating a culture of respect and dignity is a dynamic process requiring periodic reflection, adaptation, and commitment from leaders at all levels.

Critical Takeaways for Maintaining a Culture of Respect

Creating and maintaining a culture of respect in the workplace is a steady journey that requires dedication, innovation, and strategic thinking. Examining the practices and principles of organizations that have successfully created such environments can yield valuable lessons and actionable insights. The following critical takeaways highlight essential strategies to help other organizations sustain a respectful and inclusive work environment and enhance employee morale and overall company performance.

1. **Leadership is key:** The tone from the top sets the expectation for behavior throughout the organization. Leadership commitment to a culture of respect is critical to its success.
2. **Dynamic learning opportunities:** Instead of static training sessions, offer interactive and immersive learning experiences such as workshops, role-playing scenarios, and real-world simulations. These methods can be more engaging and effective in reinforcing behaviors contributing to a respectful workplace.
3. **Open communication channels:** It is essential to maintain open and safe channels for employees to voice concerns or report disrespectful behavior. This not only aids in addressing issues promptly but also reinforces the organization's dedication to a respectful work environment.
4. **Recognition and reinforcement:** Recognizing and rewarding respectful behaviors reinforces the importance of these actions and encourages their continuation. Positive reinforcement can effectively shape the organizational culture.
5. **Proactive policy evolution:** Regularly review and update company policies to reflect the latest best practices and societal changes. This proactive pathway ensures that the organization remains responsive and relevant in promoting a culture of respect.

By learning from these success stories and fundamentals, organizations can establish and nourish a culture of respect that uplifts employees. This enhances organizational performance and reputation, ensuring long-term success and a supportive work environment.

Challenges to Respect and Dignity at Work

Despite the clear benefits and progressing endeavors to advance respect within the workplace, organizations continue to encounter significant challenges that hinder their ability to implement and maintain a culture of dignity and respect. These obstacles range from deeply ingrained biases and systemic structures that perpetuate discrimination to a lack of understanding or commitment at individual and leadership levels. The complexities of workplace dynamics, amplified by the increasing reliance on virtual communication, add further difficulty in ensuring that every interaction is respected. Addressing these challenges requires policy changes and a transformation in organizational mindset and behavior at every level.

Recognizing these challenges is the first step toward mitigating their impact and maintaining a supportive, respectful workplace environment. In this section I explore the various barriers to respect and dignity at work, drawing on examples and research to illuminate the practical difficulties organizations encounter. I also discuss strategies for overcoming these obstacles, emphasizing the role of leadership in modeling respectful behavior and the importance of creating inclusion and belonging. A focused examination of these challenges aims to provide actionable insights that can guide organizations in strengthening their commitment to a culture of respect and dignity, eventually achieving more.

Four Common Barriers and Misconceptions

A significant challenge in advocating for a workplace culture of respect and dignity is overcoming common barriers and misconceptions that can undermine these efforts.

1. Belief that Respect Must Be Earned

One prevalent barrier is the belief that respect must be earned. This belief can lead to a hierarchy of respect based on seniority, accomplishments, or personal biases. This perspective can create divisions and hinder the formation of a universally respectful workplace culture. For example, junior employees may feel undervalued if their contributions are consistently overlooked in favor of senior staff.

2. Equating Respect with Agreement

Another misconception is equating respect with agreement. Some may feel that disagreeing with someone's ideas or decisions is disrespectful. This can stifle open communication and innovation, as employees may be reluctant to express differing opinions or ideas for fear of being perceived as rude. For instance, an employee might hesitate to share a new approach to a project, worrying it will offend their colleagues.

3. Addressing Unconscious Bias and Microaggressions

Addressing unconscious bias and microaggressions—subtle, often unintentional actions or comments that can diminish respect and dignity—can be challenging. These behaviors can be profoundly ingrained and require conscious effort and education to identify and overcome. For example, consistently mispronouncing a colleague's name can convey a lack of respect for their identity.

4. Failure to Recognize Diverse Communication Styles and Cultural Norms

The failure to recognize and adapt to diverse communication styles and cultural norms can also be a barrier. What constitutes respect can vary significantly across cultures, and a lack of sensitivity to these differences can lead to misunderstandings and feelings of disrespect. For instance, direct feedback may be valued in one culture but perceived as confrontational in another.

Addressing these barriers requires a commitment to education, open dialogue, and self-reflection at all organizational levels. By recognizing and confronting these common misconceptions and barriers, companies can take meaningful steps toward creating a more inclusive and respectful work environment, ultimately fostering greater collaboration and productivity.

Resistance to Change in Improving Respect and Dignity at Work

Understanding resistance to change is a critical challenge when enhancing respect and dignity within the workplace. Attempting to alter deep-rooted corporate cultures and behaviors often encounters resistance across various organizational levels. This resistance can manifest for multiple reasons, including discomfort with the unfamiliar, fear of diminished status or job security, and skepticism about the genuine commitment to change.

Resistance can be particularly potent when initiatives to improve respect and dignity challenge established norms and power structures. Employees might feel threatened by the shift towards a more inclusive and respectful environment if they perceive it as undermining their traditional roles or are not entirely convinced of the initiative's value.

Leaders play a crucial role in navigating this resistance. They can significantly ease the transition by modeling the behavior they wish to see, providing clear communication about the benefits and rationale for the changes and engaging employees in the change process. Leadership needs to listen to concerns and provide reassurance through consistent actions, reinforcing the long-term benefits of a respectful and dignified work environment. Educational programs that address the importance of inclusivity and explain how changes will be implemented can also help ease the transition, as can the establishment of feedback channels that allow employees to voice concerns and contribute ideas.

Reducing resistance to change in respect and dignity at work requires a strategic approach that combines transparency, engagement, and accountability. By taking these measures, organizations can boost a culture that values diversity and inclusion and recognizes the strength and competitive advantage such an environment brings to the company.

The Beckhard-Gleicher Change Model provides a crucial lens through which to view the dynamics of organizational change, particularly in fostering a culture of respect. As an experienced OD consultant and thought leader, I have observed that resistance to change is a common and significant barrier to cultivating this culture. In alignment with the model, successful change requires that the dissatisfaction with the current state (D), coupled with a compelling vision for the future (V) and actionable first steps (F), collectively outweigh the resistance (R). Understanding this equation illuminates how we can design strategies that address change's emotional and practical aspects. This approach not only smooths transitions but also enhances the implementation of initiatives aimed at creating a respectful workplace. By leveraging these insights, organizations can effectively navigate resistance and foster more respectful and dignified environments and, ultimately, be more successful. [36]

Conclusion

Successful organizations understand that their foundation lies not just in the products they create or the services they offer but in the people who make it all happen. Apple, under the leadership of Chief Executive Officer (CEO) Tim Cook, emphasizes that a culture of respect and dignity is the bedrock upon which they build their teams, products, and future. This approach encapsulates the essence of workplace environments where everyone is valued and respected.[37]

This chapter has elaborated on the significance of respect and dignity in the workplace, illustrating how these foundational values can be effectively nurtured and maintained through various organizational examples and leadership means. It's evident that when employees feel genuinely respected, it enhances their engagement, boosts their productivity, and strengthens their loyalty to the organization. The benefits of such a culture extend far beyond the immediate workplace, contributing to a more inclusive, equitable, and compassionate society and encouraging a positive reputation.

However, recognizing the importance of respect and dignity only marks the beginning. The true challenge—and opportunity—lies in the routine, deliberate actions taken to embed these values into the fabric of organizational life. It demands more than policy declarations or one-off initiatives; it requires a sustained commitment to live out these principles in every interaction, decision, and strategy.

Leadership must advocate for and embody these values at all levels, setting a precedent for the organization.

Let's call upon leaders, managers, and all employees to unite as champions of this cause. By actively promoting respect and dignity in daily interactions, embedding them into management practices, and holding each other accountable to these standards, we can transform the theoretical into the practical. We collectively have the power to create workplaces that are not merely productive but also profoundly human-centered, where respect and dignity are not aspirational ideals but lived realities.

Our commitment to these core values will be tested as we confront new challenges and adapt to evolving workplace dynamics. Yet, our dedication to endorsing a culture of respect and dignity will prove most critical in these moments. By prioritizing these principles in every facet of our work, we can pave the way for a future where every workplace is a model of respect, dignity, and inclusion.

Reflection Questions for Chapter Two

- How have you experienced resistance to change within your organization, particularly in initiatives to foster respect and dignity? What strategies were employed to address this resistance, and were they effective?

- Reflect on a time when a leader in your organization modeled behavior that promoted a respectful and dignified workplace. How did this leadership influence the attitudes and behaviors of employees?

- How can clear communication about the benefits and rationale for change help reduce resistance to initiatives focused on respect and dignity? Provide examples based on your personal experience or observations.

- How can educational programs and feedback channels be designed to genuinely engage employees and ensure their concerns and ideas are heard to cultivate a more inclusive work environment?

- Considering the Beckhard-Gleicher Change Model, evaluate how well your organization balances dissatisfaction with the current state, a compelling vision for the future, and feasible steps to outweigh resistance to change. What improvements can be made to this approach?

Chapter 3

Valuing Individuals and Individualism: Celebrating Uniqueness

Imagine the high-stakes world of fintech, where Emily, a junior analyst at a prestigious investment firm, uncovers a looming market crash that all senior analysts have overlooked. When she presents her findings, she faces skepticism and dismissal from her superiors, who prioritize consensus over individual insight. Instead of retreating into isolation, Emily seeks allies within the team, sharing her data and gaining support. Together, they bring the analysis to the chief executive officer (CEO), saving the firm millions and advancing a cultural shift that values individual expertise within a collaborative framework.

This story underscores the critical value of the individual within the workplace—a concept vital for innovation, productivity, and long-term success. Chapter Three delves into the intrinsic worth of each employee, focusing on how recognizing and nurturing individual talents boosts organizational performance and embeds a culture of respect and dignity. It explores strategies for identifying and leveraging unique contributions, promoting diversity of thought, and supporting personal and professional growth. By understanding these principles, leaders can create a meaningful and inspiring work environment that lays the groundwork for cohesive, high-performing teams.

Moreover, this chapter emphasizes that focusing on the individual does not exclude the importance of collective efforts but rather sets the stage for a more detailed examination of team dynamics in subsequent chapters. By first laying a strong foundation of respect and dignity at the individual level, organizations can create healthier and more effective team interactions. Through this comprehensive approach, organizations can achieve operational excellence and foster a vibrant workplace culture, ultimately unlocking the full potential of their workforce and driving sustained success.

Beyond Numbers: Seeing Employees As Whole Persons

Recognizing employees as whole persons is fundamental to leveraging the people dividend. This approach views every member of the organization not just as a worker but as a multidimensional individual. This perspective is crucial in dynamic work environments, where the well-being and engagement of employees are directly linked to achievement. Seeing beyond the numbers means acknowledging that employees bring their entire selves to work, including their personal wants and needs, concerns, and hopes.

Organizations championing this understanding tend to advance environments where trust and support flourish. This is about creating workplaces where individuals feel safe to share their ideas and struggles, knowing that their contributions will not be overlooked. It involves a commitment from leadership to invest in the overall well-being of their employees—recognizing that when people feel respected and cared for, they are motivated and loyal.

The people dividend emerges when companies shift from viewing employees as resources to partners in growth. This shift requires policies and practices that recognize and celebrate individual contributions. By doing so, organizations prove that treating employees as whole persons is smart business.

In the academic fields of organizational behavior and leadership, Dr. Linda Hill and Dr. Amy Edmondson of Harvard Business School emphasize the importance of creating environments where employees feel empowered to share their unique insights and ideas openly.[38, 39] Their research highlights the crucial role of psychological safety in fostering a workplace culture that embraces individuality. This involves promoting inclusivity and empowerment, acknowledging the diverse talents and contributions of each individual, and going beyond traditional group dynamics to enhance the organization as a whole.

Hill and Edmondson offer complementary perspectives on the concept of psychological safety, with Edmondson delving more into the individual experience within the organizational context. Her work centers on cultivating an environment where employees feel safe to express their thoughts without fear of reprisal, nurturing a culture of learning and personal innovation. By emphasizing psychological safety for individuals, Edmondson advocates for open communication, risk-taking, and personal growth within the organizational structure.

By integrating Dr. Hill's and Dr. Edmondson's insights, companies can establish a comprehensive plan that celebrates individuality and furthers a culture of innovation and resilience. However, recognizing individuality goes beyond mere acknowledgment—it requires active efforts to understand and cultivate the diverse capabilities within a team. Innovative companies often employ personalized career development plans and mentorship programs to identify and nurture each employee's strengths.

Emphasizing individuality enhances problem-solving capabilities and adaptability. When employees feel their unique perspectives are valued, they are more likely to contribute ideas to help the organization evolve. This agility is crucial for maintaining a competitive edge. Yet, achieving this level of individual recognition within a team-oriented setting presents its own set of challenges. Leaders must strike a delicate balance between celebrating personal achievements and cultivating a sense of collective identity and purpose. Successful organizations manage this by setting clear goals, aligning individual objectives with the company's broader mission, and ensuring that every contribution moves the team forward.

One powerful strategy for balancing individual and collective success is implementing cross-functional teams. By bringing together employees from different departments to work on shared projects, companies can create a collaborative environment that leverages diverse skills while aiding unity.

Despite the potential obstacles, the rewards of prioritizing individuality within a team-oriented setting are manifold. Recognizing employees as whole persons and aligning their unique strengths and aspirations with team and organizational goals is essential. It requires a thoughtful leadership stance that acknowledges each team member's diverse capabilities and personal ambitions while guiding them toward a unified vision. This alignment ensures that individual efforts contribute meaningfully to organizational objectives and create a synergy that amplifies overall team performance. By valuing individuality alongside team cohesion, organizations can strike a balance that maximizes organizational goals.

The Strategic Imperative of Personal Development in the Modern Workplace

Aligning individual aspirations with business outcomes is a vital component of organizational strategy. When employees are empowered, they feel in control of their work environment and confident in their ability to make meaningful contributions. This sense of empowerment is closely linked to personal development opportunities, enabling individuals to leverage their unique skills and talents effectively. According to a LinkedIn Learning report, 94% of employees would stay at a company longer if it invested in their career development. This insight underscores the importance of learning and skill development as central to employee satisfaction and organizational success.

Like Ken Blanchard and Spencer Johnson in their classic book *The One Minute Manager*, experts highlight the significance of empowering employees by setting clear goals, providing immediate feedback, and encouraging an environment of mutual respect.[40] These strategies enhance individual performance and contribute to creating a culture where personal growth is encouraged and valued. Furthermore, Gallup's research on employee engagement shows that organizations focusing on strength-based development can expect increased profitability, productivity, and customer satisfaction.[41] These findings suggest that when employees are recognized for their strengths and given chances to develop them further, the benefits ripple throughout the organization.

Implementing effective empowerment strategies requires leaders to adopt a growth mindset, viewing challenges as opportunities for expansion and learning. In her research on mindset, Carol S. Dweck outlines how working for a culture of growth not merely benefits individual employees but can transform an entire organization.[42] By encouraging risk-taking and learning from failure, organizations can build a resilient workforce adept at navigating the complexities of the business world.

Technology also plays a central role in facilitating empowerment and personal development. Digital platforms offer an array of resources for skill enhancement, from online courses to virtual mentorship programs. Tools like Coursera, LinkedIn Learning, and Udemy have democratized access to learning, enabling employees to pursue personal and professional development paths tailored to their interests and career goals. These platforms support individual growth and help organizations keep pace with industry trends and technological advancements.

A notable example from the engineering and medical device industry is Medtronic's Eureka program.[43] The Eureka program encourages employees across the company, regardless of their position or department, to submit innovative ideas that could transform patient care or improve business processes. This initiative demonstrates Medtronic's commitment to leveraging the diverse talents and insights of its workforce to drive innovation. Medtronic's approach exemplifies how empowerment and personal development are integrated into the fabric of the organization. Employees are given the tools and resources to enhance their skills and encouraged to think creatively and contribute ideas that can lead to groundbreaking medical advancements. This culture of innovation has led to significant developments in medical technology, enhancing patient outcomes worldwide. The success of Medtronic's Eureka program showcases the potential of empowerment to catalyze innovation within the engineering and medical device sectors. Companies like Medtronic champion a culture of continuous learning by actively seeking out employee contributions. This advances technological and medical progress and reinforces the company's position as an industry leader committed to improving human health.

Personal development and empowerment also profoundly impact mental health and well-being. A study published in the *Journal of Vocational Behavior* found that empowerment practices are positively associated with job satisfaction and negatively related to job strain.[44] By investing in personal development and creating an empowering work environment, companies can reduce turnover and increase engagement.

For empowerment and personal development to be genuinely effective, they need to be inclusive, ensuring all team members, regardless of their background or position, have access to growth opportunities. Deloitte's research on inclusive leadership shows that inclusive workplaces see up to 30% higher revenue per employee and greater profitability than competitors.[45] Inclusion in empowerment strategies ensures diverse perspectives are leveraged, enriching the organizational culture.

Empowerment and personal development are intertwined elements critical to individual fulfillment and organizational success. Businesses can cultivate a forward-thinking workforce through strategic investment in regular learning, skill development, and creating an empowering organizational culture. Expert insights, alongside persuasive statistics, underscore the multiple benefits of empowerment—from enhanced employee satisfaction and well-being to increased organizational performance and competitiveness. In an era where talent is a key differentiator, empowering individuals to grow and develop is no longer optional.

Empowering Individualism: Strategies for Effective Team Leadership and Collaboration

Individualism within team dynamics and organizational culture revolves around recognizing and appreciating each team member's unique characteristics, skills, perspectives, and contributions. It involves valuing individual autonomy, creativity, and decision-making within a collective framework. Embracing individualism means acknowledging that every team member brings a distinct set of experiences, strengths, and ideas to the table, endorsing an environment where these differences are respected and leveraged for the benefit of the team as a whole.

When managers and leaders respond to individuals, they don't just adopt a personalized approach; they create a supportive work environment tailored to each team member's strengths, preferences, and developmental needs. A personalized response may involve conducting one-on-one meetings to understand career aspirations, providing tailored feedback on performance, and offering skill development opportunities based on individual goals. By recognizing and responding to the unique needs of each team member, managers can create a supportive work environment that promotes personal growth and engagement, making them feel empowered in their role.

Managing one individual involves providing personalized support and guidance customized to that team member's specific needs and goals. In contrast, managing many individuals requires a broader perspective that considers the collective dynamics, strengths, and challenges of the entire team. Leaders must balance individual attention with nurturing a cohesive team culture.

Balancing autonomy and collaboration are critical to managing individualism within a team. While autonomy allows individuals to work independently, make decisions, and take ownership of their tasks, collaboration boosts teamwork, communication, and shared goal achievement. Influential leaders understand when to empower individuals to work autonomously and when to encourage collaboration to leverage collective intelligence and achieve team objectives.

An essential strategy for managers responding to individuals is creating personalized development plans aligned with each team member's career aspirations and skill development needs. These plans include setting clear goals, identifying training opportunities, and providing feedback to support individual growth. Tailoring development plans to the unique strengths and aspirations of team members enhances job satisfaction and overall team effectiveness.

Recognizing and celebrating individual contributions within the team is a crucial leadership strategy for managing individualism. Managers support a culture of appreciation and motivation by acknowledging each team member's unique skills, achievements, and efforts through public recognition, rewards, and advancement opportunities. Valuing individual contributions boosts morale and encourages team members to continue delivering excellence.

Influential leaders don't just prioritize open communication channels; they endorse a culture of trust and respect. This culture allows team members to freely voice their opinions, share ideas, and express concerns. By creating a culture of open dialogue and transparent feedback, managers encourage individual expression and build trust within the team. Encouraging open communication enables leaders to address particular needs, resolve conflicts, and further a collaborative work environment.

Leaders play a crucial role in managing conflict resolution effectively in response to conflicts involving individual team members. Managers can prevent escalation, restore trust, and maintain team cohesion by addressing conflicts promptly, impartially, and constructively. Strategies for managing conflict resolution in the context of individualism include facilitating discussions, seeking common ground, and mediating solutions that respect individual differences and organizational goals. Handling conflicts with sensitivity and fairness upholds a culture of collaboration and mutual understanding within the team.

Managers respond to individuals by empowering them to make decisions and take ownership of their work. Leaders instill confidence and a sense of accountability in team members by delegating responsibilities and trusting individuals to perform at their best. Empowerment and trust are essential to managing individualism effectively, enabling individuals to showcase their capabilities and contribute positively to team achievements.

Social Media, Individuality, and Organizations

In the digital age, social media platforms have emerged as powerful channels for individual expression, shaping identities and influencing cultural norms within and outside the workplace. The intersection of social media and individuality introduces a dynamic element to organizational cultures, challenging traditional norms and expectations. Employees no longer leave their personal brands at the door when they enter the office; instead, they bring their whole selves to work, including the persona they have crafted on platforms like LinkedIn, Twitter, and Instagram.

This blending of personal and professional identities through social media not only challenges organizational norms but also empowers individuals in unique ways. It democratizes the process of reputation-building, allowing employees to gain influence and establish thought leadership without relying solely on hierarchical advancement. An employee with a strong social media presence can shape perceptions and influence decisions, disrupting traditional power dynamics within an organization. For instance, an employee who actively shares industry insights on LinkedIn may become a recognized thought leader, attracting new clients and business opportunities for their company.

Furthermore, social media amplifies the voices of employees, enabling them to share their work, celebrate achievements, and express opinions more broadly than internal communication channels might allow. This visibility can breed a culture of transparency and authenticity, which are undoubtedly beneficial. However, it also poses challenges for maintaining consistency in corporate messaging and values. Organizations must navigate the balance between encouraging individual expression and ensuring that these public personas align with the company's brand and ethical standards. For example, an employee who posts controversial opinions on Twitter might create public relations issues for their employer, leading to conflicts over brand alignment and professional conduct.

The impact of social media on individuality within the workplace also extends to recruitment and retention strategies. Prospective employees often turn to social media to gauge an organization's culture and values, drawn to companies that encourage self-expression and support social causes. Similarly, current employees use these platforms to express their workplace experiences, influencing their peers' perceptions and potentially attracting or deterring future talent.

Addressing the challenges and opportunities presented by social media and individuality is not just a task but a necessity. It requires an understanding of digital culture and its implications for organizational behavior. Leaders, as the architects of organizational culture, must shepherd and actively promote an environment where individual expression is seen as an asset rather than a threat. They need to provide guidelines that encourage responsible use of social media while preserving the space for personal branding and advocacy. By doing so, organizations can leverage the power of individuality to enhance their cultural vibrancy and competitive advantage for today and tomorrow.

In essence, social media has transformed how individuals express their uniqueness and how these expressions interact with and reshape organizational cultures. It challenges leaders to rethink traditional norms, inspiring a more inclusive and adaptable pathway to harness every individual's full potential.

Case Examples of Individual Recognition and its Benefits

Recognizing individual efforts and achievements within industry-specific contexts is a key driver of organizational culture and success across sectors. By acknowledging the unique contributions of professionals within diverse industries, businesses can unleash waves of creativity and elevate customer experiences.

However, recognizing individual efforts extends beyond mere acknowledgment—it catalyzes positive change and growth within industries, showcasing the transformative power of valuing individual contributions. The impact of industry-focused individual recognition becomes evident in the evolution of organizational practices and outcomes, from technology advancements to healthcare services and sustainability initiatives to creative campaigns. Let's consider how industries leverage the recognition of individual efforts to drive tangible benefits and propel businesses toward excellence. Consider these case examples from the technology, healthcare, manufacturing, community banking, marketing, and hospitality sectors to explore how individual recognition fosters and amplifies organizational impact.

1. **Technology:** A large software company implemented a monthly recognition program that highlighted individual achievements in innovation, irrespective of the department. This initiative led to a remarkable increase in patent filings and fresh project proposals, showcasing how recognition can stimulate creativity and drive technological advancements.

2. **Healthcare:** Recognizing individual efforts in patient care led to improved patient satisfaction scores for a global healthcare provider. The organization boosted morale by honoring nurses, doctors, and support staff for their personal contributions to patient care. It enhanced the overall patient experience, demonstrating the critical role of recognition in the healthcare sector.

3. **Manufacturing:** A manufacturing company introduced a sustainability champion award, recognizing employees who contributed ideas or initiatives that significantly reduced environmental impact. The program resulted in numerous eco-friendly innovations, from waste reduction measures to energy-saving techniques, highlighting the power of individual contributions to organizational sustainability goals.

4. **Community banking:** A community bank initiated a program to spotlight employees who went above and

beyond in community service and financial education efforts. This recognition increased employee participation in community outreach programs and strengthened the connection between the bank and its local communities, underscoring the value of individual contributions to corporate social responsibility.

5. **Marketing:** At one marketing firm, individual recognition for creative projects led to a surge in unique and high-quality campaign proposals. By celebrating the creative achievements of its designers, copywriters, and strategists, the agency enhanced its portfolio and established a culture of innovation and excellence.

6. **Hospitality:** Recognizing staff members who created exceptional guest experiences at this hotel chain led to significant improvements in guest satisfaction ratings. This wasn't just about boosting morale; it was about motivating employees to provide personalized and memorable services, directly contributing to the brand's reputation for excellence in hospitality. This case exemplifies how individual recognition can elevate service standards and customer satisfaction in the hospitality industry.

Each of these case studies illustrates the profound impact that recognizing individual efforts and achievements can have on an organization. By acknowledging the whole person and their unique contributions, organizations can tap into the people dividend and create a culture of excellence that benefits employees, customers, and the bottom line.

Checklists and Tools for Recognizing Individual Contributions

Recognizing individual contributions can significantly enhance employee engagement and satisfaction. In this section, we will explore various checklists and technological tools designed to identify and celebrate employee achievements. By leveraging these resources, you can create a culture of appreciation that not only motivates employees but also aligns with broader organizational goals.

Leveraging Technology for Recognition

In the age of digital transformation and artificial intelligence, numerous technological tools and platforms offer unconventional ways to recognize employee contributions effectively. From social-recognition platforms to mobile apps designed for peer-to-peer kudos, technology facilitates timely, widespread, and impactful recognition. Companies should assess available technologies that align with their culture and recognition goals, ensuring these tools are accessible across the organization for maximum participation and impact.

Crafting Recognition Checklists

Developing a recognition checklist is a practical means for managers and leaders to ensure consistent and meaningful acknowledgment of employees' efforts. Key components might include criteria for recognition, methods of acknowledgment (public or private), frequency of recognition efforts, and a variety of recognition forms to address different achievements and milestones. This checklist ensures that no noteworthy contribution goes unnoticed and that the recognition process is equitable and inclusive.

Personalizing Recognition Strategies

Understanding individual employees' preferences for recognition is crucial. Some may appreciate public acknowledgment during team meetings, while others value a personal thank-you note or a one-on-one discussion. Tools such as surveys or feedback forms can help gather preferences and insights, enabling managers to tailor their recognition strategies effectively, thereby increasing their significance and impact.

Development Programs for Managers

Equipping managers with the right tools and training is critical for growing a recognition-rich environment. Workshops and e-learning courses on the art of effective recognition can empower managers to acknowledge their team's contributions in ways that resonate and motivate them. Training should cover the importance of timely recognition, understanding and leveraging individual differences in recognition preferences, and the impact of recognizing efforts on employee engagement and motivation.

Integrating Recognition into Performance Management

Recognition should be an integral part of an organization's performance management system, not an afterthought. Tools that integrate recognition data with performance reviews can provide a comprehensive view of an employee's contributions over time. This integration encourages a culture of sustained feedback and recognition, moving beyond the traditional annual review to a more dynamic, ongoing performance management process.

Utilizing Recognition Platforms

Recognition platforms can centralize and streamline the process of acknowledging employee contributions. These platforms often include features such as badges, leaderboards, recognition feeds, and the ability to link recognitions to specific company values or goals. When selecting a platform, consider ease of use, customization options, integration capabilities with other HR systems, and the ability to generate reports and insights on recognition activities.

Continuous Improvement and Feedback

Finally, any recognition program should include mechanisms for regular review and improvement. Soliciting employee feedback on the effectiveness and impact of recognition practices can help identify areas for refinement. Tools for collecting this feedback include surveys, focus groups, or suggestion box mechanisms. By regularly updating recognition strategies based on employee feedback, organizations can ensure these practices remain aligned with the goal of enhancing organizational success.

Incorporating structured recognition practices and leveraging advanced technological tools can revolutionize how organizations celebrate individual contributions. Businesses can cultivate a motivating work environment by crafting detailed recognition checklists, personalizing strategies, equipping managers with the right training, and utilizing comprehensive recognition platforms.

Improvement through feedback ensures that these practices remain effective and meaningful, driving sustained employee engagement and organizational excellence.

Conclusion

Leaders must see beyond the numbers and recognize employees as whole persons. This strategy aligns with ethical standards and significantly benefits organizations, including increased innovation, improved employee morale and engagement, enhanced customer satisfaction, and improved business performance.

Individual recognition should not be seen as a one-time event but rather as an ongoing effort that supports a culture of appreciation, collaboration, and growth. When employees feel valued and recognized, they are more likely to go above and beyond, contributing to organizational success. Organizations can harness the people dividend by utilizing tools such as technology, checklists, personalized strategies, training programs, integration with performance management systems, recognition platforms, and feedback mechanisms to create a culture of excellence through individual recognition. Always remember to recognize the whole person and their unique contributions—it will pay dividends.

By implementing policies and practices that value individual recognition, companies can unlock the full potential of their workforce and thrive in challenging markets. Let's remember to see and appreciate the whole person behind the employee and reap the rewards of the people dividend. Let's create workplaces where individuals can bring their whole selves to work and be recognized for their unique contributions. The results will speak for themselves—happy, engaged employees motivated to drive success for themselves and the organization.

Reflection Questions for Chapter Three

- How can organizations effectively address the challenges of transitioning from a performance-based recognition system to one that appreciates employees as whole persons?

- What game-changing tools or platforms can be utilized to recognize individual contributions through technology, and how do they impact employee engagement and morale?

- Describe the interplay between policies supporting work-life balance, career development, and individual recognition. How do these elements collectively contribute to unlocking the workforce's full potential?

- In the context of the people dividend, how can organizations measure the impact of individual recognition on overall business performance?

- What steps must leaders take to genuinely incorporate a culture of appreciation, collaboration, and growth into the organizational DNA, ensuring employees feel valued and recognized for their unique contributions?

Chapter 4
Unlocking Potential through Diversity and Inclusion

Reflecting on my experiences, I've realized that diversity, equity, and inclusion represent far more than just undeniable catalysts for organizational transformation and success; they embody a comprehensive approach to creating workplaces where every individual feels valued, understood, and integral to the collective endeavor. In navigating the business world, I've observed a fundamental transition in how these concepts are perceived—from social virtues to business necessities. This evolution marks a significant shift in how organizations navigate social responsibility. It's no longer just about fulfilling quotas or sidestepping public backlash; it's about understanding the immense potential embedded within a diverse workforce. Our discourse will extend the concepts contained in the people dividend, and by the conclusion of this chapter, you'll possess a definitive framework for unlocking the true potential of your workforce.

It's important to note that equity goes beyond equal treatment to address systemic inequalities and ensure everyone has access to the same opportunities, regardless of their background or identity. It involves recognizing and dismantling barriers that may prevent certain groups from fully participating or advancing within the organization. Committing to equity acknowledges that fairness sometimes requires different approaches and resources tailored to individuals' needs and circumstances.

Regarding inclusion, Verna Myers, a renowned advocate for diversity and inclusion, is known for her powerful insights on the importance of inclusive leadership. She famously articulated the difference between diversity and inclusion by saying, "Diversity is being invited to the party; inclusion is being asked to dance."[46] As a thought leader in this field, Myers emphasizes that true leadership goes beyond forming diverse teams—it involves actively engaging with each team member to ensure everyone feels valued and heard. Her philosophy highlights the critical roles of respect and dignity in contributing to an inclusive work environment where humanistic values are not just ideals but everyday practices.

Belonging is the idea that when individuals have a seat at the table and feel genuinely welcomed and respected for who they are, we create progress. It's been an essential addition to our framework of having people bring more of who they are to what they do. Hence, our focus in this chapter and in the people dividend is on diversity, equity, inclusion, and belonging (DEIB). In short, DEIB is about acknowledging that each person contributes a unique set of experiences, perspectives, and skills—factors that, when effectively harnessed, drive us toward business solutions that might otherwise remain undiscovered.

However, to fully realize DEIB's potential, we must deeply embed these concepts and, in addition, the notion of justice into an organization's character. Justice involves actively challenging and rectifying unfair practices and biases that permeate our organizations and society. It compels us to make internal changes and advocate for broader societal shifts toward inclusivity and fairness. Embedding justice into our DEIB efforts means actively working to correct injustices and create an environment where equality is not just an ideal but a lived reality for all.

These interconnected concepts—diversity, inclusion, belonging, equity, and justice—form a framework for guiding an environment where every individual can thrive. Recognizing and celebrating the diverse experiences and talents each person brings to the table and ensuring that they do so equitably, feeling a true sense of belonging and justice, we unlock an unparalleled capacity for creativity and problem-solving. This approach propels our organizations forward and contributes to building stronger communities.

The backlash against diversity, equity, inclusion, and belonging (DEIB) initiatives is manifesting in various sectors, especially those undergoing significant cultural shifts. One notable example can be seen in the corporate arena, where employees may feel overwhelmed or threatened by change, leading to pushback against DEIB training programs that they perceive as unnecessary or biased. In educational institutions, some faculty and students argue that an emphasis on diversity may compromise meritocracy, resulting in heated debates that blur the lines between constructive dialogue and outright resistance. To navigate this growing backlash, leaders must engage in transparent and empathetic communication, fostering an environment where employees understand the value of DEIB as a vital component of organizational success rather than a mere obligation. This approach can help dismantle misconceptions and encourage a collective commitment to embedding these principles within the organizational culture, ultimately paving the way for more sustainable and meaningful change.

Together, we will venture into the substantial domain of DEIB, discovering the strategies and actions that can transform the idea of the people dividend into an achievable reality. In an era where businesses are increasingly evaluated based on their dedication to diversity and inclusion, the ability to authentically leverage the people dividend will set apart the leaders from the followers, the innovators from the imitators. In doing so, we will forge a path to a more equitable and inclusive future and a course toward business excellence.

The Innovation Imperative

The need for innovation is deeply grounded in the principles of DEIB. These elements drive organizational creativity and enhance competitive edge. As change accelerates, HR leaders become architects in creating work environments that value diverse perspectives and inclusive practices. Without innovation, organizations cease to flourish, as they do without fully acknowledging the value of DEIB.

This innovation imperative leverages the people dividend through a work culture where DEIB is foundational to organizational resilience and expansion. For human resources (HR) professionals, promoting DEIB goes beyond compliance or ethical reasons. These values are crucial to sustainable business growth. As such, HR leaders play a crucial role in attracting a varied workforce and ensuring employees feel a sense of belonging and worth. Their efforts help create a workplace environment where everyone feels valued and rewarded, which can boost innovation.

A diversity-forward approach allows companies to spark creativity. Inclusion enhances this by valuing all voices, including traditionally marginalized ones, in decision-making processes. This synergy between diversity and inclusion can lead to groundbreaking ideas and strategies for maintaining competitiveness, the cornerstones of innovation. The people dividend, in this case, materializes as increased agility, showing that innovation through diversity and inclusion significantly drives corporate success. This is the power of diversity, and harnessing it is within our reach. Companies that embrace this plan will find themselves better equipped to navigate the complexities of business.

The business case for DEIB is supported by evidence showing significant benefits for team innovation and performance. Diverse teams offer a wealth of ideas, establishing environments where creativity flourishes and groundbreaking innovations emerge. Referencing Maya Angelou again, she fittingly noted, "It is time for parents to teach young people early on that in diversity there is beauty, and there is strength," underscoring the advantage of diverse perspectives. This is like viewing the world through a wider lens, challenging conventional techniques, and encouraging new realms of creativity and problem-solving. By adopting a diversity-forward mindset, companies can break away from traditional methods and explore new growth opportunities. This broader perspective is essential for remaining competitive.

Industry leaders such as Adobe and LinkedIn exemplify the power of diversity in driving innovation. Adobe's commitment to DEIB is evident in its achievement of global gender pay parity and efforts to address the pay gap for underrepresented minorities. LinkedIn shares its diversity data and goals transparently, regularly publishing reports to track progress and hold itself accountable. Their dedication to cultural, gender, and functional diversity results in a prolific output of next-generation products and services. This emphasis on diversity demonstrates their values and propels organizational creativity. Companies that follow their lead will likely see similar benefits.

Leadership is crucial in shaping a culture that embraces and actively seeks diversity. By creating an environment where everyone feels heard and valued, leaders set the stage for an inclusive and dynamic workplace, becoming a fertile ground for transformative ideas as employees from various backgrounds bring unique perspectives to the table. In this setting, diverse teams thrive on the strength of collective creativity, driving forward meaningful and impactful change. This collaborative atmosphere encourages open dialogue, deepens mutual respect, and cultivates a sense of belonging among all team members. Consequently, the organization benefits from a regular influx of fresh ideas and strategies, positioning itself to achieve significant success.

An innovation-centric mindset is not just beneficial; it's essential for breaking free from stagnation. Cultivating a culture that encourages curiosity and risk-taking maximizes potential and drives improvement. Embracing these values ensures that companies remain agile and forward-thinking, able to adapt and integrate technological advancements. By nurturing a diverse and inclusive workplace, organizations lay the groundwork for sustained innovation and long-term success. The journey towards integrating DEIB into the core business strategy is an essential pathway to achieving excellence.

Cultivating an Environment of Inclusion

Creating a workplace culture of inclusion is an unceasing effort that demands engagement from all organizational tiers, from the executive suite to the production floor. Beyond mere intention, it necessitates strategic action to ensure that every employee feels thoroughly valued and accepted. One central strategy to actualize this intention is implementing comprehensive learning and development programs to promote understanding and respect among coworkers. These programs, often a mix of workshops, seminars, and interactive sessions, aim to educate employees about the diverse backgrounds and perspectives their colleagues bring. Through programs that encourage and provide tools for effective communication, organizations can build cohesive and supportive work environments. In the following paragraphs, I will highlight how leaders within three distinct organizations adopted inventive measures to cultivate DEIB environments, underscoring the critical role that leadership plays in enhancing efforts toward diversity and inclusion.

First, consider the manager at a well-known tech corporation who recognized the need for a wider range of viewpoints within product development teams. Understanding that diverse perspectives drive innovation, she took the lead in creating a cross-functional team, intentionally choosing members from various departments, backgrounds, and experience levels. This effort not only brought fresh ideas to projects but also fostered a culture of learning and mutual respect among team members. This, in turn, led to the development of more innovative product solutions and boosted team morale and commitment to the company.

Similarly, at a globally recognized software firm, a leader detected a conspicuous absence of diversity amongst the company's higher echelons. Committed to reform, he unveiled a leadership nurturing program concentrated on the company's underrepresented demographics. Blending mentorship with hands-on leadership exercises, the program equipped its participants with essential skills, knowledge, and a supportive network, paving their way to career progression. By directly confronting the hurdles that impeded the advancement of certain employees, this initiative not only diversified the company's leadership profile but also underscored the organization's dedication to showcasing an equitable and inclusive environment for all.

During my time consulting at Darden Restaurants, I was truly impressed by the company's commitment to diversity and inclusion. Then Chief Executive Officer (CEO) Joe Lee, who was inspired by a diversity workshop led by Dr. Roosevelt Thomas, took action to implement his learnings. Lee made sure that all managers received training on the importance of serving diverse audiences, and he also established the most diverse board of directors in a Fortune 500 company at that time. The company's motto, "At Darden, everyone is welcome to a seat at our table," was not just a slogan; it drove comprehensive training and initiatives throughout the company. Darden Restaurants has continued to prioritize diversity and inclusion. Today, the company still boasts one of the most diverse boards of directors among Fortune 500 companies, with over 36% of its board members being minorities. This commitment to diversity is also reflected in the executive team, demonstrating the company's dedication to fostering an inclusive environment at all levels.[47]

Effectively addressing the degrees of workplace diversity requires a shift in perspective regarding leadership and decision-making processes. Leaders must not only advocate for DEIB but actively embody these principles in their actions and policies. This involves soliciting feedback from employees at all levels, ensuring that diverse voices are heard and considered in strategic decisions. Furthermore, transparent communication about the organization's diversity goals and progress toward meeting them can endow a sense of accountability and shared responsibility among all staff members, thereby reinforcing the importance of an inclusive culture. Leaders are the driving force behind these initiatives, and their commitment is crucial.

These efforts demonstrate the significant impact of integrating humanistic values into daily managerial responsibilities to support an organization's DEIB objectives. By forming diverse teams and providing development focused on reducing inequalities, leaders can directly improve the organizational culture, guiding it toward greater inclusivity. These actions benefit the individuals involved and enhance overall workplace dynamics. Upon reflection, it becomes clear that achieving comprehensive DEIB requires systematic, thoughtful efforts at every level of the organization. It is through these concerted actions that true transformation is achieved.

Leadership's Pivotal Role in Championing Inclusion

The foundation of a truly inclusive work environment is based on the recognition and active involvement of its leaders. Imagine a scenario where leaders in senior positions not only support but also demonstrate their unwavering commitment to inclusion. When executives, directors, and managers openly champion DEIB, they establish a standard for the organizational culture, indicating that DEIB is not just a policy but a fundamental value of the enterprise. This active leadership role contributes significantly to improvement and progress.

Leadership commitment to inclusion is crucial in creating an atmosphere where every individual feels valued and empowered to share their unique perspectives. It's about fostering spaces where employees feel safe to express their identities and are encouraged to contribute their diverse views. By doing so, leaders harness the power of diversity as a strategic advantage, uplifting individuals and propelling the entire organization forward.

Leaders' actions have a direct impact on the morale and performance of their teams. When leaders encourage a culture of inclusion, employees respond positively. They see their workplace as a community where their contributions are respected and valued and where they can grow professionally and personally. This sense of belonging fosters a positive work environment, leading to greater commitment and engagement.

Organizations must invest in ongoing education and training on DEIB principles to ensure that leadership at all levels can effectively champion inclusion. These programs should focus on demonstrating how diversified teams contribute to better decision-making and innovation. Organizations can create a more inclusive culture that benefits everyone by prioritizing these educational initiatives.

Additionally, leaders can promote DEIB by establishing explicit guidelines for behavior and communication within their teams. They should encourage open dialogue, seek input, and provide opportunities for diverse team members to take the lead on projects or initiatives. This approach highlights diverse perspectives and reinforces the notion that everyone's input is valuable.

Leadership's role in championing inclusion is indispensable. When leaders at every level commit to modeling inclusivity in their actions and decisions, they inspire their teams to do the same, creating a virtuous cycle of growth and enrichment. This commitment to humanistic values will drive organizations to not only be successful in their endeavors but also exemplary workplaces where people are proud to work. Through embodying these principles, leaders can transform their organizations into trailblazing and resilient communities.

Empowering Diverse Voices with Employee Resource Groups

Employee resource groups (ERGs) play a crucial role in advocating for the rights and interests of underrepresented and other groups in the workplace. Our discussion will center on improving ERGs' effectiveness by providing them with necessary support and resources. This will empower them to make meaningful and positive changes in company culture based on principles of DEIB.

The key to creating an inclusive workplace is recognizing and celebrating the unique qualities that each employee brings. By valuing diversity as a strategic asset, companies can foster an environment of respect and dignity. This type of environment encourages individuals to express themselves fully at work, which in turn lays a solid foundation for creativity and original problem-solving. Such a workplace is not just a place of work but a vibrant community where every voice is heard and every contribution is valued.

Intel, a multinational corporation, stands as a shining example of success in promoting diversity and inclusion through its ERGs. For instance, Intel's IGLOBE, the LGBTQ+ ERG, led the way in implementing a more inclusive language policy, recognizing a diverse range of gender identities across its global offices.[48] Similarly, Intel's Disability Leadership Council championed more accessible workspaces and technology, significantly improving daily operations for employees with physical and sensory impairments. These remarkable achievements underscore Intel's unwavering commitment to fostering an inclusive workplace.

As another example, a well-known retail company, Target, has been successful in promoting diversity and inclusion through its ERGs.[49] For instance, Target's Women's Business Council ERG advocated for flexible work schedules and mentorship programs, helping to advance gender equality within the company. Similarly, Target's Multicultural Network ERG introduced cultural awareness training and diverse supplier initiatives, significantly enriching the company's cultural competency and supply chain diversity. Additionally, Target's Young Professionals Network ERG developed leadership development programs and networking opportunities for early-career employees, supporting growth and engagement. These achievements underscore Target's dedication to an inclusive workplace where every employee feels valued and supported.

Embedding respect and dignity into the framework of organizational culture ensures a workplace where all employees can freely contribute, enriching the collective pool of ideas. It guarantees that every team member feels acknowledged and heard, regardless of position or tenure. This cultivates a richer sense of community and belonging, heightening engagement and informing a cohesive corporate identity. Committing to dignity and respect as core values paves the way for a dynamic and genuinely inclusive culture. It elevates each member of the team and propels the entire organization toward achieving its goals with a concerted and purpose-driven strategy. This approach benefits individual employees and enhances the collective capacity to meet challenges and seize opportunities.

HR and other leaders play a crucial role in developing these groups. They can offer leadership training specifically designed for ERG leads, equipping them with the necessary skills to effectively manage and advocate for their groups. Financial support is also essential, allowing ERGs to organize events, invite speakers, and create programs that benefit both their members and the wider company. Additionally, establishing formal channels for ERGs to communicate their insights and recommendations directly to senior management promotes a two-way dialogue that can lead to meaningful change. Implementing these measures will ensure ERGs have the resources and executive support needed to thrive and make a lasting impact on organizational culture.

The inclusion of the people dividend concept in ERGs' plans enhances their value and impact on the organization. The people dividend acknowledges that employees are more likely to reach their full potential when they feel included, fostering an environment where innovation thrives. By actively supporting ERGs and incorporating these principles into the corporate purpose, companies improve individual well-being and achieve a substantial return on investment. This approach ensures that the commitment to diversity and inclusion leads to tangible benefits for all stakeholders.

Measuring and Monitoring Progress

To effectively assess the impact of diversity and inclusion initiatives, it is essential to have a strong framework for measurement and monitoring in place. This involves understanding that comprehensively capturing the full scope of diversity and inclusion within an organization requires a strategic approach. By utilizing various metrics and benchmarks, organizations can thoroughly evaluate the effectiveness of their efforts. Setting clear and achievable goals, along with regular assessment, is crucial to ensuring that these initiatives reach their intended objectives and significantly contribute to the ongoing improvement of organizational culture. Through strategic measurement and diligent monitoring, companies can pinpoint areas that need improvement and drive progress.

The rationale behind utilizing qualitative and quantitative measures is rooted in the complexity of capturing the essence of diversity and inclusion within any organization. Quantitative data, such as demographic statistics, promotion rates, and pay equity figures offer objective insights that illuminate disparities and facilitate the tracking of progress over time. However, these numerical insights represent just one facet of the story, providing a limited perspective on the dynamics at play. Conversely, qualitative measures unveil a more profound understanding of the employee experience. Techniques like interviews, surveys, and focus groups enable the collection of personal narratives that shine a light on employees' lived experiences, imbuing quantitative data with the necessary context and depth. This ensures a thorough assessment, uncovering the mechanics and motivations behind the effectiveness or failures of diversity and inclusion efforts.

Incorporating humanistic values into this integrated technique emphasizes the organization's commitment to creating an environment where everyone feels valued. This focus on humanistic values and an inclusive workforce strengthens the organization. By combining quantitative data with qualitative insights, organizations can gain a more accurate understanding of their current situation and the necessary steps for progress. This approach addresses both surface-level issues and deeper systemic challenges, aligning diversity and inclusion initiatives with the broader mission of creating lasting change and showing respect for human dignity.

Below are distinct approaches for qualitative and quantitative analyses. These explorations will further elucidate how each method contributes to a comprehensive understanding of diversity and inclusion efforts, reinforcing the critical role of humanistic values and the pursuit of the people dividend in shaping equitable and vibrant organizational cultures. This method underscores the principle that beyond achieving mere compliance or superficial diversity targets, the goal is to nurture an organizational mission that celebrates diversity as a fundamental component of its identity and success.

Qualitative Measures of Inclusion

Understanding the impact of diversity and inclusion initiatives within an organization requires a qualitative assessment beyond mere numbers to capture the essence of workplace culture, employee perceptions, and individual experiences. Through interviews, focus groups, and surveys, this mode of inquiry allows organizations to gain deep insights into how effective their policies are, uncover any unconscious biases, and assess the level of psychological safety among employees. The open and honest communication that these methods endorse reveals the subtler aspects of inclusion—such as a sense of belonging, respect, fairness, camaraderie, trust, and dignity—and is critical to creating a genuinely inclusive environment.

Taking Starbucks as an exemplary case that highlights the significance of qualitative measures in enhancing workplace culture.[50] Known for its strong commitment to diversity and inclusion, Starbucks took the remarkable step of closing all its U.S. stores for a day to conduct anti-bias training, demonstrating its dedication to creating a welcoming and inclusive environment. This initiative is part of a larger strategy to combat racial biases and grow a culture where everyone feels they belong. Through feedback mechanisms like focus groups and forums, Starbucks actively listens to its employees, referred to as "partners," ensuring their voices are heard and acted upon. This dedication to understanding and addressing the needs and concerns of its workforce underscores the power of qualitative assessments in driving meaningful progress in diversity and inclusion efforts.

Respect is a crucial factor when assessing the positive effects of diversity and inclusion initiatives. Organizations can gauge whether employees truly feel that their opinions are respected and valued by conducting structured interviews or focus groups. This feedback can help determine the effectiveness of diversity and inclusion training in creating an inclusive environment. For example, insights from these discussions can demonstrate a cultural shift towards more respectful interactions, where individual contributions from diverse backgrounds are acknowledged and valued.

Fairness is closely linked to how equitable the workplace feels to its employees. Surveys are invaluable for gauging whether employees perceive equal access to opportunities and believe reward and recognition systems are free from bias. The feedback obtained can highlight areas for policy adjustments to accommodate the diverse needs of the workforce, eventually leading to increased satisfaction and retention, especially among employees juggling caregiving responsibilities or in need of flexible work arrangements.

Camaraderie reflects a working culture where individuals feel supported and uplifted by their peers. Insights from focus groups explicitly discussing the impact of mentoring programs or team-building initiatives reveal how these strategies can enhance a sense of community and dismantle barriers among different employee groups. Often, the success of such programs in backing inclusivity is attributed to their ability to promote mutual respect and understanding across a diverse staff.

Trust is a crucial foundation in creating an inclusive workplace. It comes from clear communication, fair decision-making, and honest leadership actions. Using tools like survey feedback systems or confidential interviews can help uncover whether employees feel comfortable expressing their concerns and believe that their responses will bring about positive changes. This level of trust fosters open discussions about diversity and inclusion, ensuring that initiatives are not just top-down directives but collaborative efforts that reflect the real needs and suggestions of the workforce. When employees see their ideas and concerns being taken seriously and leading to real changes, it strengthens their trust in the organization's commitment to inclusivity, making them feel more secure and engaged.

Dignity is another essential aspect that reflects the organization's commitment to treating every employee with respect and valuing their inherent worth. Assessing dignity in the workplace involves examining how DEIB initiatives address and prevent instances of discrimination, harassment, and microaggressions. It requires creating spaces where employees can share their experiences without fear of retribution and ensuring clear, accessible avenues for reporting issues. Training programs that educate employees on recognizing and respecting cultural differences, as well as policies that affirm the rights and identities of all employees, are critical for promoting dignity. By integrating these values into the corporate culture, organizations can maintain an environment where everyone feels respected and valued for their contributions and who they are, thereby laying the foundation for a truly inclusive workplace.

By incorporating these fundamental elements into the framework of qualitative assessment, organizations can gain a comprehensive understanding of the impact and effectiveness of their DEIB initiatives. This involves evaluating the integration of DEIB principles into various aspects of the organization, including policies, practices, and culture. By conducting a thorough qualitative assessment, organizations can identify areas for improvement and measure progress, ultimately paving the way for a workplace that not only values diversity and inclusion but also embodies these principles at its core.

Quantitative Measures of Inclusion

Quantitative analysis plays a crucial role in advancing organizational DEIB initiatives. This method uses data and metrics to assess the effectiveness of efforts aimed at creating inclusive workplaces. It helps identify successes and pinpoint areas that need improvement. Organizations can gain a comprehensive view of their DEIB progress through key performance indicators (KPIs) such as the demographic composition of the workforce, leadership diversity, employee retention, promotion rates, and pay equity assessments. In addition, evaluating participation in diversity training programs provides insights into an organization's commitment to building an inclusive culture. This is essential for establishing benchmarks and tracking the effectiveness of DEIB initiatives over time. By employing quantitative measures, organizations can objectively assess their success in harnessing this people dividend, ensuring that their DEIB policies and practices are effective in achieving their intended outcomes.

Accenture provides a great example of how using quantitative measurements can greatly improve diversity and inclusion initiatives. The consulting firm has observed a significant increase in female leadership because of targeted recruitment and development programs designed to support women's advancement. This has not only improved gender diversity at the leadership level but has also shown Accenture's commitment to DEIB. It demonstrates the tangible benefits of having a diverse leadership team.

Successful organizations understand that their foundation lies not just in the products they create or the services they offer, but in the people who make it all happen. Walmart, for example, has made significant strides in creating a more inclusive work environment through comprehensive diversity and inclusion training programs.[51] These initiatives aim to build a culture of respect and dignity, which serves as the cornerstone upon which teams, products, and futures are built. Such efforts emphasize the importance of workplace environments where everyone is valued and respected, ultimately contributing to overall organizational success.

Boston Scientific has made remarkable strides in employee satisfaction through its diversity initiatives within the medical device sector.[52] The company has consistently achieved high engagement scores over the years, reflecting its commitment to improvement and adaptation based on employee feedback. Boston Scientific's approach illustrates the successful realization of the people dividend through enhanced employee engagement and morale, emphasizing the importance of a satisfied and respected workforce for overall productivity and motivation.

Quantitative data is extremely important for reflecting on past performance and making informed decisions for the future. It helps organizations set realistic, data-driven goals and paves the way for genuine cultural change. Therefore, quantitative analysis is essential for capturing the benefits of DEIB, which is crucial for implementing a strong and impactful strategy. Managers can use these results to identify areas where DEIB strategies may need adjustments and allocate resources strategically to address any gaps. By monitoring trends over time, managers can refine their policies to better promote an inclusive culture, reinforcing the essential human values that are crucial to organizational success.

In conclusion, the strategic use of quantitative measures in DEIB initiatives emphasizes the critical role of data-driven decision-making in leveraging the people dividend. Through the examples of leading companies like Accenture, Walmart, and Boston Scientific, it becomes clear that quantitative methodologies can lead to substantial progress in creating workplaces where diversity is actively valued and leveraged for collective success. Such efforts meet immediate objectives and lay the groundwork for enduring transformation, embedding diversity and inclusion deeply within the essence of organizational culture.

Addressing Resistance Among Managers

When encountering managers who are hesitant to support DEIB efforts, it's important to approach the situation with a strategic and empathetic mindset. Understanding the underlying reasons for their resistance, which may arise from a lack of awareness, fear of change, or a misunderstanding of the benefits of DEIB, is crucial. Here are seven specific actions organizations can take to effectively address and overcome this resistance.

1. **Educate on the benefits:** Provide evidence-based training and share success stories showcasing the tangible benefits of a diverse and inclusive workplace, such as enhanced creativity, better decision-making, and improved employee satisfaction and retention.

2. **Set clear expectations and accountability:** Incorporate DEIB goals into the broader organizational objectives and key performance indicators for managers. This will ensure that meeting these goals is considered a professional responsibility, thereby reducing resistance and holding managers accountable for advancing an inclusive workplace.

3. **Regular feedback and performance reviews:** Use these tools to monitor progress and ensure compliance with DEIB initiatives, reinforcing the importance of meeting these expectations.

4. **Introduce rewards and consequences:** Implement recognition programs and other incentives for managers who actively promote and support DEIB. Conversely, outline clear repercussions for those who do not engage in these efforts.

5. **Promote openness and dialogue:** Create a safe, non-judgmental environment for managers to voice their concerns and hesitations. Workshops or roundtable discussions can facilitate sharing experiences and challenges related to DEIB.

6. **Demonstrate leadership commitment:** Lead by example, demonstrating an unwavering commitment to diversity and inclusion through actions and decisions and serving as a role model for all managers.

7. **Encourage peer support and mentorship:** Establish a peer support system or mentorship program where managers can learn from colleagues who have successfully navigated and implemented DEIB initiatives.

Addressing resistance is not merely a hurdle to overcome; it's a critical step towards unlocking the full potential of the people dividend and implementing successful DEIB initiatives. When managers buy into these efforts, they play a crucial role in shaping an organizational culture that values diversity as a critical driver of innovation, creativity, and employee engagement. This alignment is essential for tapping into the unique perspectives and talents of every employee, thereby enhancing the organization's ability to solve complex problems, innovate, and connect with a diverse customer base. Organizations can unlock the vast reservoir of employee potential by understanding resistance and encouraging an inclusive environment, transforming diversity from an abstract ideal into a tangible asset.

Leadership strategies are paramount in this endeavor. Leaders must not only advocate but also embody these values in their daily actions and decision-making processes. This includes being proactive in recognizing and addressing biases, backing policies and practices that promote equality, and ensuring that all voices within the organization are heard and valued. Furthermore, leaders can facilitate mentorship programs and career development opportunities to empower underrepresented groups within the company. Through such strategies, leaders signal a genuine commitment, setting the tone for the entire organization and paving the way for the successful realization of the people dividend. This comprehensive course ensures that diversity and inclusion are not just peripheral concerns but are central to the organization's purpose and operational strategy, leading to a more vibrant, creative, and competitive business.

Integrating these actions can mitigate resistance and encourage a shift in mindset toward recognizing the value of diversity and inclusion. Education, accountability, dialogue, and demonstrating leadership are all critical components in transforming reluctance into active support and championing a more inclusive organizational culture.

Conclusion

In concluding this chapter, it's critical to reflect on the many means required to harness the actual value of diversity in the workplace. The innovation imperative highlights the undeniable link between diverse perspectives and enhanced creativity and problem-solving abilities. Organizations can support innovation by tapping into a broader range of experiences and ideas, driving growth and competitiveness in an increasingly complex global market.

Cultivating an environment of inclusion is not merely about meeting quotas or ticking boxes. It's about creating a space where everyone feels valued, heard, and empowered to contribute their best work. This involves dismantling barriers to participation and ensuring equitable opportunities for growth and advancement. Such an environment benefits individuals and enriches the organization, contributing to a more dynamic, agile, and resilient business.

Leadership plays an indispensable role in championing these values. Leaders set the tone for organizational culture, and their commitment to diversity and inclusion can inspire widespread change. By modeling inclusive behaviors, advocating for equitable policies, and holding themselves and others accountable, leaders can break down systemic inequalities and nurture a culture of belonging. Their vision and actions are crucial in steering the organization toward a more inclusive future.

Empowering diverse voices through ERGs offers another powerful strategy for advancing inclusion. ERGs provide platforms for underrepresented groups to share their experiences, insights, and recommendations with the broader organization. These groups can drive awareness, advocate for change, and support professional development, contributing significantly to the organization's diversity and inclusion goals.

Measuring and monitoring progress is essential to understanding the impact of these efforts and guiding future strategies. Through a combination of quantitative and qualitative measures, organizations can gain a comprehensive view of their progress toward becoming more inclusive and diverse. This ongoing assessment helps identify areas of success and opportunities for improvement, ensuring that diversity and inclusion efforts remain aligned with evolving goals and challenges.

Addressing resistance among managers is a critical step in this process. Organizations can transform skepticism into support by educating, setting clear expectations, and furthering a culture of openness and dialogue. It's about shifting mindsets and demonstrating the tangible benefits of a diverse and inclusive workplace—not only for employees but also for the business.

Unlocking the people dividend through diversity and inclusion requires a sustained, strategic effort. It's about leveraging all employees' unique strengths and perspectives to create a more visionary, adaptable, and successful organization. As we progress, the principles outlined in this chapter serve as a blueprint for building more inclusive workplaces where everyone can thrive. This is not just a strategic imperative for organizations seeking to excel in a diverse world but also essential for fostering innovation and resilience, ensuring that organizations can respond effectively to the complexities of ever-evolving markets and ultimately drive sustainable success.

Reflection Questions for Chapter Four

- How can we ensure that our diversity and inclusion initiatives go beyond meeting quotas to genuinely creating an environment where everyone feels valued and empowered?

- What steps can leaders take to model inclusive behaviors and advocate for equitable policies within the organization?

- In what ways can ERGs be leveraged to support professional development and drive awareness of diversity and inclusion issues?

- How can we effectively measure and monitor the progress of our diversity and inclusion efforts to ensure they are aligned with our evolving goals and challenges?

- What strategies can we implement to address and transform resistance among managers regarding diversity and inclusion initiatives?

Chapter 5:

Beyond Production Elements – People at the Core

Treating people as mere elements of production can manifest in various forms within an organization. One clear example is stringent performance management systems that focus solely on output, often at the expense of employee well-being or job satisfaction. In these cases, employees are assessed purely on their productivity or achievement of specific targets, with little regard for their development, creativity, or input into the processes in which they are involved. Another example is the minimization of training and development opportunities. Companies may view training as a cost rather than an investment, limiting employees' growth and potential contributions to the organization.

Taylorism, or scientific management, introduced by Frederick Winslow Taylor in the early twentieth century, plays a significant role in shaping this perspective.

Taylorism emphasizes efficiency and productivity through the meticulous study of workflows and tasks, which are then optimized and standardized. Employees are assigned specific tasks with precise instructions on how to perform them, reducing the need for skilled labor and making the workers easily replaceable. While it led to unprecedented increases in efficiency and productivity in industrial settings, Taylorism is criticized for treating workers like cogs in a machine, ignoring their fulfillment.

I've seen the transformative power of a human-centered approach while leading organization development (OD) and human resources (HR) teams within several large corporations. One instance that stands out was a major restructuring phase where we shifted our focus from managing performance metrics to employee development. By implementing a mentorship program and endorsing a culture of thoughtful learning, we saw a significant boost in employee engagement and innovation. This shift in perspective led to employees feeling respected and empowered. This experience underscores the potential benefits of investing in the workforce beyond traditional productivity metrics.

Conversely, I've also seen the detrimental effects of neglecting this human-centered method. In one company, a particular boss would routinely go around inspecting who was in their office and who wasn't; not out of curiosity but as a form of surveillance. This created an environment of mistrust and significantly dampened morale. The leadership's overemphasis on output and rigid performance management systems resulted in a disengaged workforce, as was evident in feedback from employee opinion polls. The lack of engagement meant that people wouldn't put in any extra effort; they would merely go through the motions, mirroring the manager's bed-check behaviors. These experiences serve as potent reminders that treating employees as integral and valued members of the organization rather than mere production elements is essential for long-term success and sustainable growth.

Understanding the value of human capital and moving away from treating employees as production elements is not just a trend but a necessity for growing a thriving organizational environment. By investing in employee development and building a culture of trust and respect, organizations can tap into the full potential of their workforce. Human-centrism drives innovation and engagement and ensures sustainable growth and long-term success. In this chapter, we continue to emphasize the importance of an organization's most valuable resource: its people. This chapter highlights that while technology, products, and processes are crucial for organizational success, human capital is the primary driving force behind any company's achievements. Understanding and investing in the workforce fosters a positive organizational culture and sets the stage for competitive advantage in the marketplace.

Shifting Perspectives: Valuing People Over Processes

The transition to a more people-focused strategy in organizational management highlights the shift from traditional performance evaluations to more dynamic, supportive interactions that encourage growth and development. Moving away from annual review processes, which often emphasize past performance, organizations are increasingly adopting responsive feedback systems. These systems promote regular interactions between managers and employees, enhancing personal development and adaptability. This approach aligns with evolving market demands, advocating for individual career growth while bolstering organizational resilience.

The influential works of authors such as Marv Weisbord, Dick Beckhard, Warren Bennis, and Doug McGregor have played a significant role in reshaping organizational cultures to prioritize human dignity, participation, and intrinsic motivation. These thought leaders have argued that for organizations to be truly productive, they must create environments that respect human dignity and foster participation. They have advocated for management methods based on the belief that employees are intrinsically motivated (Theory Y, as proposed by McGregor) and have emphasized that these methods are more successful than those assuming employees need strict oversight (Theory X). This shift towards a management philosophy that values a culture of trust and respect represents a significant departure from traditional hierarchical models. The approaches of Weisbord, Beckhard, Bennis, and McGregor emphasize democratic governance, regular feedback, and open communication.

As a manager in a technology firm, I saw firsthand how implementing a strong feedback system transformed our team dynamics. By holding weekly one-on-one meetings and providing feedback on projects, I offered timely support and guidance. This approach improved individual performance and fostered a sense of ownership and engagement within the team. Regular interactions also enhanced my listening abilities as I became more attuned to my team members' needs and concerns. As a result, employees increasingly reported feeling "heard," which boosted their morale and commitment. This improved communication helped us stay agile and responsive to the fast-paced demands of the tech industry, ultimately driving both personal and team loyalty.

Embracing this people-centered approach signifies a broader shift towards "A New Philanthropy" within businesses.[53] This redefines corporate responsibility towards employees, communities, and the environment and champions the idea that organizations can be financially successful while also making positive contributions to society—challenging the traditional view that profit and social responsibility are mutually exclusive. This philanthropic approach highlights the growing recognition that long-term success is closely linked to the well-being of both people and the planet, which brings technology and sustainability into the discussion. While technology can increase efficiency, it should complement rather than replace human effort, highlighting ethical considerations in preserving job security and employee welfare. Furthermore, integrating sustainable practices into this human-centered framework demonstrates how organizations can lead ethically. By adopting environmentally friendly technologies and sustainable operations, companies can support planetary health and enhance the well-being of their employees and community. This comprehensive approach integrates human-centered leadership, technological innovation, and sustainability and envisions a future where businesses are essential contributors to well-being and environmental stewardship.

The shift towards a people-focused strategy in management signifies a departure from traditional hierarchical models to more dynamic, supportive interactions that prioritize growth and development. Emphasizing humanistic values, this new perspective recognizes the importance of environments where employees feel valued and motivated. The concept of the people dividend underscores that investing in employee well-being and personal development yields significant organizational benefits. Businesses can enhance individual and collective performance by integrating sustainable practices and ethical considerations into this framework, further positioning companies as vital contributors to well-being and environmental health and reinforcing their role in driving positive change.

A New Philanthropy

Building on the foundation of viewing the workforce as more than mere cogs in the industrial machine, we transition to a discussion on a new philanthropy within the organization. This shift reflects changes in internal management practices and embodies a broader transformation in how businesses perceive and enact their roles in society. Just as recognizing the total value of employees encourages a more personal and human-centered organizational culture, today's philanthropy in business extends beyond traditional corporate social responsibility (CSR) models, engaging more deeply with communities and public needs. This evolution towards a more integrated model of giving back highlights the parallels between the internal valuing of human resources and the external commitment to societal well-being, marking a significant chapter in the narrative of corporate responsibility and ethical business practices.

The New Philanthropy concept originated in the evolving understanding of corporate responsibility and the role businesses play in society. Historically, philanthropy was often seen as a form of charity, where companies would donate funds or goods without much involvement in the broader collective issues. However, during the late twentieth and early twenty-first centuries, there was a significant shift towards more strategic and integrated approaches to philanthropy. Influential thinkers like Michael Porter and Mark Kramer introduced concepts such as "shared value," which argues that businesses can generate economic value in a way that also produces value for society by addressing its challenges. This marked a move from traditional CSR to a more comprehensive and impactful corporate engagement with societal issues.

Philanthropy is often misconstrued as being solely about donating funds or goods. However, its true essence is love for humanity, expressed by corporations in various forms. In evolved corporate strategy, philanthropy has evolved far beyond the traditional scope of merely giving away funds or goods. It has transformed into a multifaceted means emphasizing sustainable impact and meaningful engagement with civil issues. Leading companies now adopt a broader perspective on philanthropy, viewing it as an integral element of their social responsibility initiatives. This shift reflects a deeper understanding of philanthropy as an expression of a company's values and a commitment to making a positive difference in the world. By integrating philanthropic efforts with their core business strategies, organizations contribute to social progress and build stronger relationships with customers, employees, and communities.

The conception of philanthropy as a mere financial transaction is giving way to models that prioritize active involvement and long-term partnerships. Companies are leveraging their unique resources, expertise, and networks to tackle complex social challenges, ranging from education and healthcare to environmental sustainability and social justice. These efforts often involve collaboration with non-profits, government agencies, and other stakeholders to maximize impact and ensure that the initiatives address genuine needs. This allows businesses to apply their innovations and problem-solving skills to benefit society while aligning with their strategic objectives.

The shift towards the New Philanthropy also influences internal management by fostering a culture that values and invests in employees as crucial stakeholders. Instead of treating employees solely as resources to maximize profit, organizations now prioritize their well-being. This is in line with concepts like shared value, where companies acknowledge that the prosperity of their workforce directly impacts overall business success. Internally, this is reflected through responsive feedback systems, opportunities for professional development, and initiatives promoting work-life balance. By integrating ethical considerations and sustainable practices into daily operations, organizations create environments that improve employee satisfaction and productivity, and contribute positively to societal and environmental outcomes. This approach emphasizes a commitment to human-centered values, highlighting the idea that the success of a business is closely tied to the well-being of its people and the communities it serves.

The New Philanthropy concept directly relates to the people dividend by emphasizing the intrinsic value of investing in human capital within organizations. By aligning philanthropic efforts with core business strategies, companies address civil needs and enhance employee engagement and satisfaction. Integrating sustainable and human-centered values into management practices underscores the belief that a company's success is deeply connected to the prosperity and fulfillment of its employees. Eventually, this leads to a positive cycle where empowered employees drive more significant innovation and performance, creating a substantial people dividend that benefits the organization and the broader community.

Leadership and HR Driving the Change

The shift toward people-centered management represents a significant change in how businesses operate and succeed. While traditional models emphasize production efficiency and cost minimization, contemporary philosophies recognize that employees are the key drivers of innovation and long-term success. Human Resources often leads people-centered initiatives, but the entire organization must embrace these principles for real transformation to take place. Every department, from Operations to Finance, needs to incorporate a people-centered approach into their daily practices and decision-making processes.

Leadership should model inclusive and supportive behaviors to ensure that valuing people is a priority at every level. When all team members understand and embrace a people-centered approach, it creates a cohesive culture where everyone is invested in the success and well-being of their colleagues. This collective ownership not only strengthens people strategies but also drives a unified effort toward achieving broader organizational goals. To integrate managerial accountability into the people-centered management strategy, it's crucial to ensure that leaders at all levels are responsible for fostering a positive and inclusive work environment. Here's how you can do it.

Attracting Talent: Building a Magnetic Organizational Culture

Organizations must cultivate a magnetic culture that resonates with potential employees to create an environment that draws top talent. This involves articulating a clear, captivating vision and values that align with the aspirations of high-quality candidates. Managers should be accountable for communicating and embodying these values, ensuring that their teams reflect the company's commitment to employee well-being, diversity, and career growth opportunities. Leaders and HR professionals are essential in showcasing the company's commitment to these principles and are key attractors in the competitive job market.

Onboarding: Creating a Seamless Integration Process

Effective onboarding practices are crucial for integrating new hires into the company culture and setting them up for success. A structured onboarding program that includes mentorship, training, and clear communication can significantly enhance new employees' sense of belonging and reduce turnover rates. Managers must actively participate in onboarding by providing steady support and feedback, ensuring new hires feel welcomed and valued from day one. HR must ensure that the onboarding process reflects the organization's people-centered credo.

Employee Engagement: Fostering a Motivated Workforce

Engagement is vital for a productive workforce. It's important for leaders to prioritize creating an environment where employees feel valued and recognized for their contributions. This can be achieved through regular feedback, transparent communication, and opportunities for meaningful work. Managers should be responsible for maintaining high engagement levels within their teams, using metrics such as employee satisfaction surveys to track progress and areas for improvement. Engaged employees are more likely to be committed to the company's goals and motivated to go above and beyond.

Career Development: Investing in Employee Growth

The development of career paths within the organization is crucial for retaining talent and ensuring long-term success. HR should regularly implement learning and professional development programs that allow employees to expand their skills and advance their careers. Managers need to take an active role in identifying and nurturing potential in their team members, facilitating access to development opportunities, and tracking their growth. By investing in their workforce's futures, companies commit to their employees' personal and professional growth.

Retention Strategies: Maintaining a Stable Workforce

To retain skilled employees, organizations need to go beyond offering competitive compensation. They should prioritize creating a supportive work environment that includes flexible work arrangements, wellness programs, and a focus on maintaining a healthy work-life balance for employees. It's essential for managers to be evaluated based on their ability to keep turnover rates low within their teams and to consistently assess and address employee satisfaction and needs. Additionally, leadership needs to actively reinforce the organization's commitment to prioritizing the well-being and growth of its employees.

Performance Management: Aligning Individual and Organizational Goals

Performance management systems should align individual goals with organizational objectives. Managers are responsible for setting clear, achievable goals for their team members, providing regular feedback, and conducting performance reviews that emphasize development and growth. This alignment will ensure that all employees work towards common objectives, enhancing overall efficiency and effectiveness.

Leadership Development: Cultivating Future Leaders

Developing future leaders is crucial for sustaining organizational growth. Managers should be responsible for identifying leadership potential within their teams and mentoring emerging leaders, providing opportunities for them to develop their skills and take on new challenges.

Leadership development programs should be a joint effort between HR and current leaders, ensuring a pipeline of capable and motivated future leaders.

By building managerial accountability into these areas, organizations can ensure that their people-centered initiatives are thoroughly embodied at all levels, driving sustainable success and a positive workplace culture. How does this revised plan align with your goals?

Trailblazers of Transformation

When highlighting trailblazers in people-centered management, one must tread carefully between recognition and hero worship. Creating lists of exemplary leaders and companies comes with its own set of risks and rewards. On the one hand, such lists can illuminate best practices and offer concrete examples of success, providing a roadmap for others to follow. On the other hand, there's the danger of oversimplifying complex achievements and contributing to a hero-following mentality, which can overshadow the collaborative efforts and systemic changes these transformations often require.

Despite the risks, the main purpose of sharing these stories is not to put individuals or organizations on an unattainable pedestal but to inspire and prompt action at all levels of an organization. By exploring the experiences of these pioneering leaders and companies, we can discover valuable insights into the principles and practices that drive significant change. These narratives are not just stories but powerful catalysts that can fuel your journey toward creating a thriving, people-centered workplace where every employee can contribute to and share in the organization's success.

Three Trailblazing Leaders

Lisa Su (AMD)

Transformation: Since taking on the role of CEO in 2014, Lisa Su (voted 2024 Chief Executive of the Year by *Chief Executive Magazine*) has orchestrated a remarkable transformation at Advanced Micro Devices (AMD).[54] Under her leadership, the company has shifted its focus towards high-performance computing and graphics technologies, driving innovation and growth in these key areas. Su's leadership style emphasizes a culture of openness, collaboration, and technical excellence, reinvigorating AMD's corporate culture.

Impact: Under Lisa Su's visionary leadership, AMD has experienced significant growth and renewal. By realigning its business strategies to emphasize cutting-edge technology and customer-centric values, the company has demonstrated the profound impact of prioritizing both technological advancement and the well-being of its employees. This serves as a powerful example of the potential for positive transformation within any organization through a focus on innovation and people-centered management.

Mary Barra (General Motors)

Transformation: As the CEO of General Motors, Mary Barra has been instrumental in transforming the company's culture by promoting transparency, diversity, and innovation.[55] She encourages open communication across all levels of the organization and has taken bold steps toward creating a more inclusive workplace. Under her leadership, GM has launched several initiatives to improve diversity and inclusion, such as its commitment to becoming the most inclusive company in the auto industry.

Impact: Under Barra's leadership, GM has seen a notable increase in employee engagement and morale. She has championed various programs aimed at professional development and career growth, ensuring that employees feel valued and supported. Additionally, Barra has spearheaded GM's transition towards sustainable and electric vehicle technologies, aligning the company's operational objectives with its dedication to social responsibility and environmental stewardship. This alignment has not only enhanced GM's market position but also reinforced its commitment to people-centered management and innovative growth.

Indra Nooyi (PepsiCo)

Transformation: During her tenure as CEO of PepsiCo, Indra Nooyi championed initiatives focused on sustainability, diversity, and employee empowerment. She implemented the "Performance with Purpose" strategy, which aligned business goals with social responsibility and employee well-being.[56] This approach emphasized financial performance and underscored the importance of making positive contributions to society and the environment.

Impact: Indra Nooyi's leadership and innovative approach significantly enhanced PepsiCo's employee satisfaction and retention rates. She introduced programs that promoted professional development, diversity, and inclusion, ensuring a supportive and dynamic work environment. Additionally, Nooyi's strategic initiatives led to substantial progress in the company's sustainability efforts, including reducing water usage, improving recycling rates, and developing healthier product lines. These efforts set new standards for corporate responsibility within the industry and demonstrated that profitability and social good can go hand in hand.

Three Trailblazing Companies

Zappos

Transformation: Zappos has built its entire corporate culture around delivering happiness to both customers and employees.[57] They emphasize a flat organizational structure, where employees are empowered to take initiative and are encouraged to bring their whole selves to work.

Impact: The company's unique principle has created a highly engaged workforce, exceptional customer service, and strong business growth. Zappos is often cited as a model for creating a positive and dynamic workplace culture.

Spotify

Transformation: Spotify's workplace culture emphasizes autonomy, mastery, and purpose.[58] The company promotes a flexible work environment, frequent learning, and a strong emphasis on diversity and inclusion.

Impact: This outlook has helped Spotify attract top talent, maintain high levels of employee engagement, and drive innovation in the competitive tech industry.

Unilever

Transformation: Unilever has made significant strides in creating a people-centered culture through its Sustainable Living Plan, which integrates employee well-being with broader social goals.[59] The company promotes flexible working arrangements, comprehensive health and wellness programs, and strong support for learning and development.

Impact: Unilever's initiatives have led to high employee satisfaction and retention rates, alongside enhanced productivity and innovation. Their commitment to sustainability and employee welfare has strengthened their global brand reputation.

In celebrating these trailblazers of transformation, it is crucial to remember that the objective is not merely to applaud individual or organizational achievements but to draw inspiration and actionable insights from their journeys. The stories of Satya Nadella, Mary Barra, Indra Nooyi, and companies like Zappos, Spotify, and Unilever highlight the profound impact of placing people at the core of business strategies. Their successes underscore the tangible benefits of endorsing a culture of empathy, inclusivity, and sustained growth—principles that any organization can adopt to drive meaningful change.

The ultimate takeaway is that true transformation is a collective endeavor rooted in systemic change and shared values. Organizations can cultivate environments where employees feel valued and empowered by learning from these exemplary leaders and companies. This will enhance individual satisfaction and engagement and propel the organization toward sustained success and innovation. Let these narratives serve as both a guide and an inspiration, encouraging you to create a thriving, people-centered workplace.

Reflective Strategies for HR and Other Business Leaders

When considering integrating people-centered management principles demonstrated by industry trailblazers into your organizational culture and practices, it is essential to reflect on specific actions or policies that could be implemented or improved to better support employee well-being and engagement. This effort is key to ensuring that all management levels are held accountable for leading an inclusive and supportive work environment, which might involve instituting performance evaluations that measure managers' commitment to people-centered values and practices.

Fostering an irresistible organizational culture that captivates and retains top talent involves emphasizing and elevating the unique aspects of your organization's vision, values, and practices. These elements have the power to draw in exceptional candidates and inspire current employees. To ensure consistent enhancement in employee engagement and satisfaction within your teams, it's important to explore potential metrics, feedback systems, and regular check-ins. These invaluable tools offer actionable insights into employee morale and enable pinpointing specific areas for improvement.

Lastly, developing and supporting future leaders within your organization necessitates strategic implementation of mentorship opportunities, professional development programs, and leadership training. These strategies will help identify and nurture the next generation of leaders, ensuring a robust leadership pipeline. By contemplating these strategies, you can apply the transformative lessons of industry trailblazers to your organizational context, promoting thoughtful consideration and actionable change.

Integrating Psychological Safety into Organizational Dynamics

Amy Edmondson's concept of psychological safety is a foundational pillar in creating an organizational environment where diversity, inclusion, and philanthropy can thrive.[60] Psychological safety, coined by Edmondson, refers to the belief that individuals won't be punished or humiliated for speaking up with ideas, questions, concerns, or mistakes. This notion is critical in advancing open dialogue and frequent feedback, which is essential for a truly inclusive and progressive workspace.

In organizations that are successful in creating psychologically safe environments, employees feel empowered to express their true selves at work. This empowerment fosters an environment where diverse thoughts and ideas can be freely shared without fear of facing negative consequences, leading to increased innovation and collaboration within the organization. Such organizations often make substantial strides in philanthropic initiatives, as they can freely exchange ideas on how to positively impact society.

Similar experts in the field, like Brené Brown, emphasize vulnerability and empathy in leadership, supporting Edmondson's assertions. Brown's research highlights how leaders who openly express their vulnerabilities instill trust and openness within their teams. This reasoning amplifies creativity and efficiency and reinforces the organization's commitment to diversity and inclusion by valuing every employee's unique perspective.

Introducing psychological safety into the workplace allows companies to effectively transition from well-doing to well-being. When employees feel safe, they are more willing to engage meaningfully in their work and pursue initiatives aligning with their values and the organization's philanthropic goals. This alignment is crucial for creating a productive, genuinely satisfied, and mentally healthy workforce.

The success stories of companies that have advanced their diversity, inclusion, and philanthropy goals underscore the importance of psychological safety. These trailblazers have shown that when employees feel respected and valued for their unique contributions, the organization thrives. Their achievements demonstrate the effectiveness of psychological safety in directing an environment conducive to innovation and social responsibility.

The work of authors like Simon Sinek, who places great emphasis on the significance of "Why" in leadership, adds valuable insights to the discussion on psychological safety. Sinek's emphasis on purpose and belonging aligns with Edmondson's framework by proposing that when individuals comprehend their role and importance within a broader mission, they become more engaged and open to taking interpersonal risks.

Incorporating psychological safety principles significantly enhances an organization's people dividend. This concept underscores the substantial returns gained by nurturing an environment where everyone feels secure and respected. When employees are confident that their voices will be heard without fear of negative consequences—whether sharing novel ideas, expressing concerns, or admitting mistakes—they engage more fully with their work. This heightened engagement creates a rich culture, directly contributing to the organization's social and financial capital. The people dividend highlights the tangible benefits of investing in a psychologically safe workplace, illustrating how such an environment is vital for individual well-being and advancing the organization's mission and values.

Conclusion

As an HR executive, I've experienced the profound personal growth and fulfillment that comes from valuing people over processes. Early in my career, I was focused on optimizing workflows and achieving productivity targets. However, a transformative moment came when I chose to prioritize team well-being over rigid deadlines during a particularly challenging project. The results were not just astounding in terms of improved morale and innovation but also in terms of my own professional and personal growth. This shift in perspective has not only made me a better leader but has also enriched my life.

In shifting perspectives, it's clear that placing value on people creates a more resilient and adaptive organization. Our team members are no longer cogs in a machine; they are dynamic contributors whose diverse skills and insights drive our success. Emphasizing human elements supports a culture where everyone feels valued and motivated, enhancing collaboration and creativity.

This shift towards valuing people extends into a new philanthropy discussed earlier. It's not just about corporate social responsibility; it's about embedding genuine care for our employees into our organizational DNA. By investing in relevant learning opportunities, mental health support, and work-life balance initiatives, organizations see a tangible return on investment in loyalty, reduced turnover, and higher employee engagement levels.

Leadership and HR are significant in driving this change. We've moved from a command-and-control style to one that encourages empowerment and trust. By modeling inclusive behavior and maintaining open communication, leaders set the tone for a workplace where everyone feels safe to express their ideas and take risks. This, in turn, can lead to breakthrough innovations and a more decisive competitive edge.

Trailblazers of transformation within organizations have shown us the way forward. Whether in leadership roles or not, these individuals inspire others by embodying the values we strive for. Their stories of overcoming challenges through collaboration and empathy are potent reminders of what can be achieved when prioritizing people.

Integrating psychological safety into organizational dynamics has been a game-changer. It's not just about creating a safe space for employees to voice their thoughts without fear of retribution; it's about building a culture of trust and respect. This has led to more honest discussions, faster problem-solving, and a culture where learning from mistakes is encouraged rather than stigmatized. Psychological safety isn't just a buzzword; it's a fundamental component of a thriving workplace that makes everyone feel valued and secure.

Reflecting on these changes, it's evident that the journey toward valuing people over processes is not a one-time initiative but a long-term commitment. It's a continuous effort to listen, adapt, and evolve. We've learned that by focusing on the human aspects of our work, we build a foundation for sustainable success. This sustained commitment reassures our team members and stakeholders that we are dedicated to their well-being and growth and confident in the positive impact it will have on our organization.

Looking ahead, the challenge lies in maintaining and deepening this commitment. Our core principle remains steadfast as we navigate an ever-changing world: people are our greatest asset. By continually investing in their growth and well-being, we ensure that an organization survives and thrives. Embracing a people-centered value system will fundamentally reshape organizations. It will bring teams closer together, drive innovation, and fortify resilience. By focusing on the well-being and growth of team members, companies will create cultures where everyone feels valued and motivated to contribute their best. This shift will improve internal dynamics and enhance overall performance and competitive edge. I am proud to be part of this movement and excited for the future we are creating together, knowing that our collective efforts will continue to drive success across various industries.

Reflection Questions for Chapter Five

- How does shifting perspectives from valuing processes to valuing people impact organizational success?

- In what ways can new philanthropic approaches contribute to a more people-centered organization?

- How can leadership and HR effectively drive transformative changes within an organization?

- What strategies can be implemented to integrate psychological safety into organizational dynamics?

- Reflect on a time when you experienced or observed a people-centered change in a workplace. What were the outcomes, and how did it affect the organizational culture?

Chapter 6:
Creating a Culture of Integrity

Establishing a culture of integrity is crucial for any organization's long-term success. Far from being just a buzzword, integrity serves as a significant competitive advantage, often determining whether an organization thrives or falters. Take the example of Wells Fargo, where unethical sales practices led to a major scandal in 2016. The creation of millions of unauthorized accounts severely damaged customer trust, resulted in billions in fines, and tarnished the bank's reputation.[61] This case vividly illustrates the severe consequences of disregarding integrity and highlights its essential role in achieving sustainable success.

Imagine an organization where every action echoes its core values, trust is the currency of everyday transactions, and ethical behavior is encouraged and rewarded. Leaders in fast-paced business environments must transcend mere rhetorical commitments to integrity and genuinely integrate it into the very fabric of their organizational culture. This demands a deliberate and strategic plan, ensuring that stated values are consistently manifested in actions and that transparency and sincerity become the norm rather than the exception. Such genuine integration, led by the leaders of the organization, can help build the trust and loyalty necessary for long-term success. This journey toward embedding integrity is not just about the organization but also about personal growth for leaders, empowering them to lead with authenticity and inspire their teams.

Creating a culture of integrity requires unwavering dedication and strategic effort. Leaders must ensure that integrity permeates every layer, influences every decision, and is prevalent in every interaction among team members and within the broader organizational context. This environment is not merely utopian but a tangible reality achievable with the right strategies and commitment. Central to this mission is the people dividend, which posits that investing in integrity-driven practices results in significant returns. When integrity is embedded at all levels, it benefits the organization's bottom line and fosters a sustainable, thriving business culture.

As detailed in my first book, *Integrity by Design: Working and Living Authentically*, the foundation of integrity involves understanding its impact on the entire business ecosystem. Even minor instances of deception can erode trust, lower morale, and eventually affect the bottom line. At the core of integrity-led organizations lies a commitment to vulnerability and accountability. Embracing vulnerability enables leaders to promote open communication and trust, essential elements of an integrity-driven culture. In this chapter, we will explore how vulnerability can be a strength, fostering a more genuine and collaborative workplace.

Cultivating a culture of accountability ensures that everyone within the organization takes responsibility for their actions and aligns their behaviors with the company's ethical standards. Upholding integrity in the workplace may present challenges, but with strategic and genuine conviction, it is possible to create a thriving environment where integrity is the cornerstone of success.

Instilling integrity into the core of an organization is not a one-time effort but an ongoing commitment requiring dedication and strategic action. By developing a culture where integrity guides every decision and interaction, leaders can set new standards for excellence. The journey towards creating an integrity-driven environment may be challenging, but the rewards are undeniable.

As we progress in this chapter, we will delve into insights and practical advice on cultivating an environment where integrity is the guiding star, directing every action and decision. For instance, implementing transparent communication channels and encouraging open dialogue can ensure that all employees feel heard and valued. This conviction empowers leaders to build a culture that upholds integrity and thrives because of it. Moreover, it helps every employee bring more of who they are to what they do, enabling them to bring their best selves to their work.

By embedding integrity at the root, organizations can set new benchmarks for operating with ethical principles. We aim to embrace integrity as a principle and as the foundation of organizational life. This approach paves the way for a future where ethical behavior and authenticity are celebrated and integral to every facet of business. Committing to integrity is not just a short-term fix but a long-term strategy to guarantee the organization's survival and prosperity. This chapter builds upon the foundational ideas explored in *Integrity by Design: Working and Living Authentically* and seeks to unravel the complexities of developing cultures steeped in integrity.

The Foundation of Integrity

At the heart of a thriving organization is a culture steeped in integrity, a characteristic that must emanate from its leaders. This isn't about policy manuals filled with do's and don'ts but about living and working authentically each day. It starts with understanding that integrity is the consistency between words and actions, the basis upon which trust is built. Trust, in turn, fuels the engagement and productivity that drive stellar results.

Leaders must be the standard bearers of integrity, demonstrating unwavering commitment to their values in every decision and action. This commitment becomes the guiding light for the organization, cultivating an environment where every team member feels personally responsible for upholding its standards. It's about creating a space where honesty is encouraged and mistakes are viewed as opportunities for growth and learning. This culture of openness encourages the expression of novel ideas and taking calculated risks without fear of undue criticism or punishment.

For example, consider Jane, a manager at a mid-sized tech company. Jane is known for her transparency and ethical decision-making. Recently, her team was working on a project with tight deadlines. During a critical phase, Jane discovered an error that could delay the project. Instead of pushing the team to overlook the mistake in favor of meeting the deadline, Jane chose to address it head-on. She called for a team meeting, openly discussed the issue, and collaboratively worked with her team to find a solution. Jane's decision to prioritize integrity over speed demonstrated her commitment to ethical standards. She used this moment as a teaching opportunity, explaining the importance of maintaining quality and honesty even under pressure. This action resolved the immediate problem and reinforced the team's trust in her leadership.

Implementing a culture of integrity requires more than just verbal commitment; it demands concrete actions and structures that support ethical behavior. This includes establishing clear policies, providing regular training on ethical issues, and setting up mechanisms through which employees can report unethical conduct without fear of retribution. A vital part of this process is the regular review and adjustment of these policies and practices to reflect the evolving ethical challenges within and outside the organization.

Recognition and reward systems also play a crucial role

in reinforcing a culture of integrity. When leaders consistently recognize and reward integrity in action, not just results, they send a powerful message about what is truly valued within the organization. This could mean acknowledging an employee who lost a business opportunity because they refused to compromise on their ethical standards or celebrating a team that prioritized doing the right thing over meeting a deadline.

Lastly, fostering a culture of integrity means investing in relationships and communication. Leaders should strive to create an environment where feedback is freely exchanged and employees feel heard and understood. This involves regular, open discussions about the organization's values, the ethical dilemmas faced, and how they align with day-to-day operations. Such conversations help normalize integrity as a core aspect of the organizational identity, making it a lived experience rather than a set of abstract principles.

By incorporating these practices, organizations can establish a strong foundation of integrity that improves their reputation and provides a solid base for long-term success. A culture grounded in integrity attracts top talent, retains dedicated employees, and fosters enduring relationships with customers and partners. It cultivates a resilient organization that can confidently navigate challenges. Integrity serves as both a strategic advantage and a driver of sustained performance and growth. How can embracing integrity shape the future of your organization?

The Implications of Deception in Business

Integrity is the foundation of success, especially in today's global business environment where personal and professional boundaries often intersect. Building trust and credibility is essential, and this can be achieved through authentic leadership and a steadfast commitment to ethical standards. Companies that prioritize these values are more likely to thrive in the long term, avoiding the lure of short-term gains through sheer greed and deceit.

The Theranos scandal serves as a powerful example of the destructive consequences of corporate greed and deceit. The company's systematic misrepresentation of its capabilities created a web of overstatements and falsehoods that ultimately resulted in a catastrophic loss of trust. The trust that had been fundamental to the company's success was shattered virtually overnight, leaving behind a trail of disillusionment among stakeholders, including investors and customers.

Surveys highlight a troubling trend of workplace misconduct, with a significant number of employees witnessing unethical behavior. Recent research by LRN Corporation, which specializes in ethics, regulatory compliance, and corporate culture, reported by Business Wire, indicates that globally, one-third of respondents observed misconduct or unethical behavior in the past year, including harassment.[62] This widespread dishonesty underscores the urgent need for leaders to address deceitful behaviors decisively, as ignoring such actions erodes trust and undermines workforce morale and effectiveness.

The Arbinger Institute's book *Leadership and Self-Deception* emphasizes the importance of committing to transparency and accountability for healthy organizational dynamics.[63] The book explores how self-deception can blind leaders to their shortcomings and perpetuate harmful behaviors within their teams. Leaders can create a more transparent and accountable workplace by recognizing and addressing these issues. This is crucial because low morale significantly affects the benefits of the people dividend; a demotivated workforce cannot fully engage in humanistic management principles, thereby stifling growth.

The consequences of deception are serious, as it can disrupt teamwork within an organization and make genuine collaboration challenging. This toxic environment can hinder leaders' efforts to create a culture of respect and motivation, which are crucial for achieving organizational objectives. Without trust as a foundation, it becomes difficult to establish cohesive and high-performing teams. Once trust is lost or damaged, it is hard to restore.

Organizations committed to humanistic management, as emphasized by the people dividend, value each team member and prioritize integrity and transparency. Deceptive practices undermine trust and hinder the achievement of these principles. To cultivate a culture of honesty, leaders must actively discourage deceit and promote open communication. This will build a stronger, more cohesive team and enhance overall organizational effectiveness by ensuring that all members feel valued and trusted.

The necessity of a united effort to eliminate dishonesty is

underscored in this discussion, highlighting the importance of collaborative action among leaders and team members. This emphasis calls for practical steps to encourage a culture of honesty and openness within organizations. Promoting transparent communication, implementing ethical guidelines, and safeguarding whistleblowers are essential in confronting deceptive practices. These recommendations provide a clear roadmap for leaders aiming to create an environment where integrity is prioritized. By drawing attention to the relationship between ethical management and human values, this approach advocates for a leadership style that acknowledges the worth of each team member, fostering mutual trust and authenticity while effectively reducing dishonesty.

The Core of Integrity-Led Organizations

An organization thrives on the strength of its integrity, which is nurtured by authentic leadership. Authentic leadership, in brief, refers to the alignment of thoughts, words, and actions. This principle goes beyond written policies and requires a daily commitment to honest professional conduct. Integrity is the coherence of skills and qualities that builds trust, driving engagement, productivity, and outstanding results.

Leaders must exemplify integrity by grounding their actions and decisions in a strong set of values. This unwavering commitment paves the way for the entire organization, fostering a culture where everyone takes personal responsibility for upholding high ethical standards. Such an environment promotes transparency and turns mistakes into learning opportunities, encouraging innovation by ensuring employees feel comfortable sharing their ideas and taking calculated risks.

Leaders must translate their words into actions to instill integrity within an organization. This includes establishing clear policies, providing regular ethics training, and creating channels for reporting misconduct without fear of retaliation. For instance, regular workshops on ethical dilemmas can help employees confidently navigate complex situations. Importantly, these practices and policies should be adaptable, evolving to address new ethical challenges as they emerge. The value of integrity is further amplified through appropriate recognition and incentives. Celebrating courage and ethical decision-making—sometimes even over business gains—underscores the organization's real priorities. Recognizing an individual's decision to uphold ethical standards, even at the cost of a lucrative deal, sends a powerful message about what the organization truly values.

Promoting a culture of integrity also demands investment in robust communication and relationships. It calls for an organizational climate where feedback flows freely and every voice is prized. Leaders should regularly facilitate dialogues about the organization's values, ethical challenges, and alignment with daily operations. These discussions help embed integrity into the core of organizational life, transitioning it from an abstract idea to a tangible practice. For instance, managers can set a powerful example by openly discussing their decision-making processes and encouraging team members to share their perspectives on ethical dilemmas.

Adhering to these approaches enables organizations to solidify their foundation of integrity, significantly elevating their reputation and forming a durable basis for enduring achievement. A consistent commitment to integrity strengthens internal cohesion and attracts stakeholders who value ethical practices. For instance, Marriott International is well known for its dedication to ethical practices and social responsibility, which has helped it build a strong reputation and foster customer loyalty.

An organization that is firmly rooted in integrity is like a sturdy ship that can weather any storm and set sail towards sustainable success. It does so by nurturing trust and loyalty among all its stakeholders over the long haul. When leaders make integrity a top priority, they are not just building a successful organization, they are paving the way for a future where ethical conduct is the rule rather than the exception, leaving behind a legacy of excellence.

The Influence of Vulnerability on Integrity

Dr. Kristin Neff, a pioneer in self-compassion research and an associate professor at Austin's Department of Educational Psychology at the University of Texas, emphasizes the importance of vulnerability in cultivating a compassionate and resilient organizational culture.[64] A colleague of Brené Brown at the same university, Neff has significantly contributed to our understanding of how vulnerability and self-compassion intersect within personal and professional realms. According to her research, vulnerability involves acknowledging our imperfections and embracing our shared human experience, which encourages genuine connections and ethical behavior within organizations. Neff argues that recognizing our vulnerabilities is not a sign of weakness but a courageous step toward personal and professional growth. This perspective encourages leaders and employees to embrace their limitations and take responsibility for mistakes—key elements of practicing integrity.

For Neff, the essence of integrity involves choosing compassion over criticism, opting for what is right over what is convenient, and embodying values rather than merely declaring them. In an organizational context, this means creating a culture where leaders are accountable for their actions and transparent about their challenges and uncertainties. It is in this space of vulnerability that trust is built and solidified.

Integrating Neff's insights into organizational culture requires creating and maintaining an environment where vulnerability and self-compassion are recognized as strengths. This involves encouraging team members to share their thoughts and feelings, even when doing so feels risky or uncomfortable. Such a culture supports integrity by making it safe for individuals to align their actions with their values and take responsibility for mistakes. This openness fosters growth as teams learn from their experiences and adapt in meaningful ways.

In addition to supporting a culture of vulnerability and self-compassion, organizations can benefit from structured programs and training emphasizing these values. Workshops and seminars led by experts on vulnerability and self-compassion can help team members develop a deeper understanding of these concepts and how to apply them in their daily work lives. These programs can provide practical tools and strategies for managing stress, improving communication, and enhancing overall well-being, supporting a more ethical and cohesive organizational environment.

Furthermore, leaders who embody the principles of vulnerability and integrity create a ripple effect throughout the organization. When leaders demonstrate self-compassion and vulnerability, they model behavior that encourages others to do the same. This builds trust and increases a sense of psychological safety, where team members feel secure in expressing their ideas and concerns. In such an environment, innovation thrives, as individuals are more willing to take risks and share creative solutions.

By integrating these insights into organizational culture, companies can build robust frameworks for ethical behavior and human connection. These frameworks support the personal growth of individual team members and the collective advancement of the organization. Organizations that prioritize vulnerability and self-compassion are better positioned to navigate challenges and achieve long-term success.

Intertwining the concepts of integrity and vulnerability as championed by Neff offers a profound blueprint for building organizations that thrive on genuine human connection and ethical behavior. Leaders bear the quintessential responsibility of being exemplars of integrity. The adage "actions speak louder than words" rings especially true here. A leader's commitment to truth and transparency sets a powerful precedent for the entire team. Ethical leadership involves making decisions that reflect moral strength and inspire confidence.

Cultivating a Culture of Accountability

Accountability is essential for organizational success. Establishing a culture of accountability goes beyond simply following rules; it involves integrating integrity into all aspects of an organization's activities. When leaders prioritize accountability, they create an environment where ethical behavior is not only expected but also valued. This culture motivates employees to take responsibility for their actions and propels the organization to achieve its goals with integrity.

However, transitioning from abstract principles to concrete practices requires deliberate action. Leaders play an integral role in this transformation by setting the tone and exemplifying the values they wish to instill. By adopting specific, actionable steps, leaders can create a workplace where accountability thrives. Such a culture enhances individual performance and strengthens positive outcomes. The following strategies provide a roadmap for leaders to create an environment where integrity and authenticity flourish, ensuring that accountability becomes a shared value within the organization.

Steps to Maximize a Culture of Accountability

1. Lead by Example

Leaders should embody the ethical standards and behaviors they expect from their team members. This includes maintaining honesty in all communications, being transparent about decision-making processes, and demonstrating respect for all individuals. By doing so, they cultivate a culture of trust and inspire their teams to uphold these standards in their actions.

2. Promote Open Communication

Creating open, honest communication channels encourages a culture where team members feel valued and heard. Leaders should facilitate regular forums for feedback, encourage dissenting opinions to drive innovation, and ensure that communication lines are always open. This openness helps build a foundation of trust and mutual respect within the organization.

3. Implement Accountability Systems

Accountability systems should be implemented to ensure ethical practices are followed at all levels. This may include setting up mechanisms for anonymous reporting of unethical behavior, regular audits of business practices, and clear consequences for violations of ethical standards. Leaders must ensure these systems are applied fairly and consistently.

4. Encourage a Learning Environment

A commitment to education and ethical training underscores the importance of integrity within the organization. Leaders should encourage ongoing learning by providing resources and training that help employees understand ethical dilemmas and the expected standards of conduct. This also includes learning from mistakes in a constructive manner, turning them into opportunities for growth.

5. Recognize and Reward Ethical Behavior

Acknowledging and rewarding acts of integrity reinforces the value placed on ethical behavior. Leaders should publicly celebrate instances where employees demonstrate moral courage or make tough decisions based on ethical principles. This boosts morale and encourages others to act similarly in future situations.

6. Practice Empathy and Understanding

Demonstrating empathy involves acknowledging the challenges and pressures that employees may face and offering support. Leaders should strive to understand their team members' personal and professional struggles, offering guidance and assistance when needed. This builds a supportive environment that nurtures integrity.

7. Pursue Transparency in All Endeavors

Transparency is critical to growing trust and integrity. Leaders should make organizational decisions, policies, and practices accessible to all employees. This includes being open about the successes and failures of the organization, which promotes a culture of honesty and accountability. Through transparency, leaders can encourage a sense of ownership and community among team members.

Cultivating a culture of accountability is a multifaceted endeavor that demands commitment and purposeful action from leadership. By leading by example, promoting open communication, implementing accountable systems, encouraging a learning environment, recognizing and rewarding ethical behavior, practicing empathy, and pursuing transparency, leaders can lay the foundation for a robust ethical culture. These strategies are not just about preventing misconduct but creating an environment where trust and integrity are the norm.

The benefits of such a culture extend well beyond mere compliance. In environments where employees feel supported and motivated, loyalty grows stronger. Cultivating a culture of accountability is a strategic investment in the organization's future. By championing these principles, leaders can inspire their teams to uphold exemplary standards of conduct, fostering both individual and collective excellence.

Challenges to Upholding Integrity in the Workplace

Despite their best intentions, leaders and team members may face situations that challenge their commitment to integrity. These challenges can include financial pressures, competitive demands, personal biases, and fear of retribution for speaking out against unethical behavior. It is crucial to address these obstacles directly to develop an ethical culture. Strategies such as creating robust support systems, ensuring that ethical considerations are integral to decision-making processes, and cultivating an environment where long-term benefit is valued over short-term gains are vital.

Navigating the precarious waters of ethical dilemmas in the workplace requires a steadfast commitment and a nuanced style. Every organizational decision concerning financial management, client relationships, or internal policies should be scrutinized through an ethical lens. Too often, the pressure to meet quarterly targets or achieve market dominance can cloud judgment, leading to compromises that may provide short-term gains but undermine long-term integrity. Leaders must remain vigilant, ensuring that ethical considerations are part of the conversation and essential in shaping business strategies.

The fear of retribution is a significant barrier to maintaining organizational transparency and integrity. Employees who witness unethical practices often remain silent, worried about the potential backlash or negative implications on their career progression. Cultivating an environment where whistleblowing is protected and encouraged is imperative. Leaders must emphasize that reporting unethical behavior is supported and is a responsibility all team members share. Organizations can empower employees to speak up without fear of retaliation by implementing robust protection measures and anonymous reporting systems.

Personal biases and ethical blind spots present a complex challenge. Everyone has their own values and preconceived notions, which can unconsciously influence decision-making processes. Organizations must prioritize diversity and inclusion as a key component of corporate social responsibility and a strategic imperative for ethical decision-making. By encouraging diverse viewpoints in decision-making, companies can reduce the risks associated with personal biases.

Competitive pressures often push individuals and organizations to their ethical limits, tempting them to cut corners, misrepresent capabilities, or engage in unfair practices. Reinforcing the principle that integrity should never be compromised for competitive advantage is essential. This involves setting clear ethical guidelines for competitive strategies, establishing open communication channels with competitors, and advocating for fair competition practices within the industry. By championing ethical competition, leaders can uphold their organization's integrity while setting a standard for the entire industry.

Finally, sustaining an ethical culture in the face of constant change demands persistent effort and vigilance. As organizations evolve, new ethical challenges will inevitably arise. Keeping integrity at the core of organizational change means regularly revisiting ethical policies, adapting them to new contexts, and engaging in dialogue about what is important. Leaders must ensure that ethical practices are integrated seamlessly into daily operations without overwhelming team members. Through persistent dedication to ethical excellence, organizations can build resilience against ethical challenges and shepherd a culture of integrity that withstands the tests of time and change.

Rewarding Ethical Behavior in the Workplace

Recognizing ethical behavior in the workplace involves more than just acknowledging it; it's about integrating ethical actions and decisions into the organization's reward system. This can be done in various ways, such as publicly acknowledging ethical behavior in company meetings or providing intrinsic rewards that contribute to a positive work environment and personal fulfillment for employees who consistently uphold the company's ethical standards. These rewards serve two main purposes: they affirm the significance of integrity within the company culture and inspire other employees to model ethical behaviors.

Embedding Ethical Behavior into the Organizational Framework

To effectively highlight and reward ethical behavior, a structured plan is necessary. First, organizations must clearly define ethical behavior within their context, which involves upholding the company's values and demonstrating leadership in challenging situations. These behaviors should be quantifiable and aligned with the overall business strategy to ensure that they contribute to ethical and business objectives.

Ensuring Transparency and Fairness

Second, it's essential to ensure that the process of recognizing ethical behavior is transparent and fair. This transparency helps to reinforce trust within the organization, showing that recognition is based on merit and alignment with ethical standards rather than favoritism or politics. Creating a committee or task force dedicated to overseeing ethics recognition can help achieve this transparency, providing a balanced and impartial perspective on what merits acknowledgment. Transparent reporting mechanisms can enhance the people dividend by clearly communicating how ethical performance metrics are evaluated and the positive impacts they have on the organization. This demystifies the process and emphasizes that ethical behaviors are systematically recognized and appreciated.

Consistent Communication and Education

Lastly, embedding the practice of recognizing ethical behavior into the corporate culture necessitates consistent communication and education. This involves regular ethics training sessions, workshops on decision-making, and open forums for discussing ethical dilemmas. By weaving ethics into the company's daily narrative, employees are reminded of its importance. They are more likely to act in ways that prioritize the company's ethical standards, knowing their actions contribute to a positive and supportive workplace environment.

Organizations can further solidify their foundation of integrity by adopting a comprehensive strategy to recognize ethical behavior, including implementing the people dividend. This practice celebrates those who uphold ethical standards and sets a precedent for the type of conduct that is valued and encouraged within the company. The people dividend is not just about extrinsic rewards but about creating a workplace where ethical behavior leads to intrinsic satisfaction and collective success.

As Mahatma Gandhi once said, "The best way to find yourself is to lose yourself in the service of others." This quote accentuates the essence of the people dividend: true fulfillment and purpose come from contributing positively to the community around us. In the workplace context, ethical behavior creates an environment where individuals feel connected and appreciated, driving personal and organizational growth. By embedding ethical behavior into the organization's fabric, companies reward integrity and cultivate a culture of trust, collaboration, and sustainable success.

Strengthening Organizational Integrity

Creating an organization's integrity culture requires a multifaceted approach, starting with establishing an official integrity agreement. This document outlines the organization's commitment to honesty, responsibility, and ethical conduct, setting a clear standard for all members to follow. By defining expected behaviors and requiring employees to review and sign the agreement, the organization lays a strong foundation for ethical practices. Regular updates to the agreement will ensure that it stays relevant and capable of addressing new challenges.

An integrity agreement is a long-term commitment to ethical behavior, distinguishing it from annual ethics training modules. While the integrity agreement is a proactive pledge by employees to consistently uphold core principles like honesty and responsibility, annual ethics training serves as a refresher course on company policies and scenarios. Both tools are crucial yet serve different roles in promoting integrity within the workplace.

Transparent communication channels are another key element in fostering an ethical environment. These channels enable open conversations about the organization's values and provide safe spaces for employees to report unethical actions. Unlike traditional ethics hotlines, these platforms encourage ongoing dialogue, building a culture of trust and respect. Ensuring multiple anonymous and confidential channels are in place, such as suggestion boxes and online platforms, is essential. Regular promotion of these channels and training managers on handling reports appropriately further strengthens this system.

Performance metrics must incorporate integrity-based evaluations to embed integrity into organizational culture. This means assessing not just the outcomes achieved by employees but also how they are achieved. Evaluating behaviors such as honesty, accountability, and fairness highlights the importance of integrity in professional success. Clear criteria for these metrics, regular performance reviews, constructive feedback, and recognition of high-integrity employees are vital components of this process.

Continuous training and development focused on integrity are essential. Training should cover ethical dilemmas, honest communication, and decision-making aligned with organizational values. Workshops that provide practical tools for maintaining integrity in challenging situations and encourage reflection on personal and organizational values can bolster a culture of integrity. Regular sessions, expert insights, practical exercises, and real-world scenarios aid ongoing development, while evaluating and improving training programs ensures they remain effective.

Implementing these measures fosters an environment

where integrity is paramount. Such an environment enhances workplace satisfaction, builds a strong reputation, and contributes to long-term success. By embedding these principles into their culture, an organization can develop robust frameworks for ethical behavior and human connection. These frameworks support both individual growth and collective organizational advancement. Prioritizing integrity enables organizations to navigate challenges effectively and embrace change.

Combining integrity with vulnerability ultimately creates a blueprint for building organizations grounded in trust and ethical behavior. Leaders have the critical role of exemplifying integrity through truth, transparency, and authentic leadership, setting a powerful example for their teams. Making legally sound and morally commendable decisions strengthens this commitment, fostering a resilient and ethical organizational culture.

Conclusion

Integrating ethical practices within an organization's fabric is not merely a modern trend but necessary for cultivating a sustainable and prosperous business environment. By fostering a culture of integrity, businesses can enhance trust, collaboration, and overall satisfaction among employees. Establishing clear ethical guidelines, encouraging open communication, and embedding integrity evaluations into performance metrics collectively contribute to a robust framework that upholds ethical standards and recognizes those who exemplify them. Consistent training and development further solidify these values, ensuring employees can navigate ethical dilemmas and make decisions that align with the organization's core principles.

The role of leadership cannot be overstated in this journey toward an ethical paradigm. Leaders who demonstrate transparency, honesty, and vulnerability set a precedent that ripples through the organization, inspiring their teams to mirror these behaviors. By prioritizing ethical decision-making and fostering an environment where integrity is celebrated, leaders can cultivate trust and mutual respect. This not only enhances the organization's internal culture but also strengthens its external reputation, ultimately driving long-term success and resilience in an ever-evolving business landscape. Through a dedicated commitment to ethical practices, organizations can lay the foundation for lasting growth and a profound positive impact beyond the workplace.

Reflection Questions for Chapter Six

- What does integrity mean to you personally, and how do you see it manifesting in your daily work?

- In what ways can you encourage open and honest communication within your team or organization?

- How do you ensure that your actions align with your values and the organization's ethical standards?

- What steps can you take to improve accountability and responsibility within your role?

- Can you recall a situation where you faced an ethical

dilemma at work? How did you handle it, and what was the outcome?

Chapter 7:

Implementing Humanistic Values in Leadership

Consider one of my clients, a tech startup experiencing rapid growth. Despite having a pioneering product and a highly skilled team, the company faced high turnover and declining employee morale. Enter their new chief executive officer (CEO), Sarah, known for her humanistic leadership approach. Rather than focusing solely on metrics and performance evaluations, Sarah chose a different path. She dedicated her first month to personally engaging with each team member, uncovering their aspirations, challenges, and unique contributions.

Sarah's strategy was straightforward yet transformative: listening, empathizing, and acting upon the insights gathered. She introduced flexible work hours—a rarity in startups—to accommodate employees' personal lives and established regular one-on-one meetings to foster open communication. She created a recognition program to celebrate individual achievements and contributions. Gradually, the cultural shift became palpable. Employees felt valued and respected, leading to increased satisfaction and a renewed sense of purpose. Innovation thrived as team members became more willing to share ideas and collaborate.

Empathy, trust, and respect can fundamentally transform an organization's culture. This chapter delves into the powerful connection between a company's success and the growth, well-being, and satisfaction of its employees. It underscores that when leaders prioritize the human aspect—acknowledging each person's unique contributions and nurturing their potential—they unleash unparalleled levels of engagement, innovation, and achievement.

This chapter explores how leaders like Sarah can embody and promote humanistic values within their organizations, cultivating the people dividend. Through practical strategies and real-world examples, I demonstrate how embracing empathy, trust, and respect can transform organizational culture. The intrinsic link between robust organizational performance and the growth, well-being, and fulfillment of its members is highlighted throughout, serving as a testament to the power of humanistic leadership. When leaders prioritize the human element, they unlock unprecedented levels of engagement, innovation, and success.

The urgency for a leadership paradigm that deeply respects and nurtures human values has never been greater. With employee burnout and disengagement at record highs, leaders must adopt a style that is both effective and profoundly humanistic. This chapter offers a practical and actionable blueprint for leaders eager to integrate core human values into their management philosophy, thereby unlocking the people dividend. In this organizational state, fostering human potential drives unparalleled growth and success. The transformative power of humanistic leadership is not just a theory but a tangible reality that inspires and motivates leaders to make a meaningful difference.

My Journey into Humanistic Leadership

My path into humanistic leadership and organization development (OD) was profoundly influenced by Charles Seashore, a mentor whose insights into group dynamics and interpersonal relations have left a lasting impact on my approach to leadership. Seashore's commitment to understanding the intricate fabric of organizational behavior and his deep empathy for individual needs and aspirations laid a strong foundation for cultivating a leadership style that values individuals at every level. His spouse and collaborator, Edith Whitfield Seashore, along with Dr. Darya Funches, further enriched my understanding of humanistic values during my time at The American University in Washington, DC, where I studied under members of NTL, the legacy of pioneering social psychologist Kurt Lewin. These personal experiences and connections make the journey into humanistic leadership more relatable and engaging for the audience.

In addition to Seashore's perceptiveness, the enduring wisdom of Abraham Maslow seamlessly integrates into my leadership philosophy. Notably, Seashore informed me that he was a client of Maslow's. Maslow's vision for fulfilling human potential—addressing each person's innate needs for belonging, esteem, and self-actualization—resonates deeply with the essence of humanistic leadership. Beyond his renowned hierarchy of needs, Maslow's contributions to the human potential movement and his pioneering ideas in positive psychology offer rich insights into nurturing environments where everyone feels genuinely valued, deeply understood, and motivated. Moreover, his later work on self-transcendence emphasizes connecting with a greater purpose, galvanizing leaders to inspire their teams toward meaningful and altruistic pursuits. The intellectual synergy between Seashore's and Maslow's credos champions nurturing environments, encouraging personal growth, peak experiences, and realizing one's fullest potential.

My experiences with organizations such as the United Farmworkers Union and the American Red Cross instilled enduring humanistic values in me. Growing up in a working-class family, attending parochial school, and attending church every Sunday helped cement these values. They deepened further when my wife Cathy and I served as Peace Corps volunteers in the Solomon Islands, giving me a profound appreciation for the dignity of life. I carried these values into the workplace, where they became particularly significant during my time at the National Labor Relations Board, my first "real job." Here, interactions ranged from dealing with highly compensated attorneys defending conglomerates to meeting minimum-wage earners who had been denied the right to organize. These experiences paved the way for me to carry these humanistic values into profitable companies where financial growth was often the primary focus.

My journey into humanistic leadership was not without its challenges. Early in my career, despite my firm belief in the potential and goodness inherent in people, my ego often obstructed my path. My need to assert authority or prove my competence overshadowed my ability to listen and empathize with my team, leading to strained relationships and missed opportunities for collaboration. However, through self-reflection and feedback from trusted mentors and colleagues, I began to recognize the importance of humility and its profound impact on leadership. As I evolved from a manager into an executive, I consciously worked on setting aside my ego to connect genuinely with and understand those I led. This journey of personal growth, marked by humility and a commitment to continuous learning, allowed me to see the immense value that each individual brings to the table, further fueling my dedication to championing an environment where everyone can thrive. It's never too late to embrace humanistic leadership.

The Significance of Humanistic Values in Leadership

"Leadership is not about being in charge. It is about taking care of those in your charge."

– Simon Sinek[65]

Humanistic values are not just lofty ideals but practical tools that can enhance managerial and leadership effectiveness. Empathy, for instance, is not just about understanding and sharing the feelings of others but also about taking tangible actions. A manager might notice that one of their employees seems unusually distant and disengaged during meetings. Instead of reprimanding them for lack of participation, the manager schedules a one-on-one meeting to check in on their well-being. This act of empathy not only boosts an individual's morale but also reinforces a culture of care and attentiveness within the team.

Integrity, another fundamental value, involves honesty and strong moral principles. Leaders who demonstrate integrity build credibility and earn respect from their teams, which is vital for long-term success. Imagine a company facing a financial shortfall where cost-cutting measures are necessary. Rather than making unilateral decisions, the CEO holds a transparent meeting with all employees, explaining the situation and seeking input on potential solutions. This approach ensures that employees understand the challenges and feel involved in decision-making, significantly enhancing trust and collective problem-solving abilities.

Respect means recognizing and valuing the inherent worth of each individual, regardless of their position or background. In a diverse workplace, a leader can celebrate multicultural events and encourage employees to share their cultural traditions and experiences. This promotes inclusivity and shows respect for the diverse backgrounds of team members. Such actions contribute to a harmonious and collaborative work environment where everyone feels valued and included.

Compassion involves showing kindness and a willingness to help others, which is crucial for creating a supportive and caring work environment. For example, if an employee's family member falls seriously ill, requiring them to take an extended leave of absence, a compassionate manager would immediately approve the leave and organize a support system within the team to cover the employee's duties. This ensures the employee can focus on their family without worrying about work. Compassionate leadership grows loyalty and reduces turnover, leading to greater organizational stability.

Fairness entails making impartial decisions and treating everyone equally, which helps to create a just and equitable workplace. A fair manager ensures that all performance reviews are based on objective criteria and documented performance metrics rather than personal biases or office politics. This approach promotes a transparent and fair assessment process, leading to increased employee satisfaction and trust. Fairness in leadership helps to reduce conflict and foster a sense of justice and equality within the organization.

Authenticity means being true to oneself. Authentic leaders inspire trust and loyalty by consistently aligning their actions with their words. For example, a leader might openly share their career challenges and mistakes during a team-building session. By being vulnerable and authentic, the leader encourages team members to be more open about their own experiences, fostering a culture of transparency and mutual support. This authenticity strengthens relationships and boosts employee engagement and commitment.

Finally, empowerment involves granting employees the freedom and authority to make decisions and take ownership of their work. For instance, a project manager may assign substantial decision-making authority to their team members, urging them to devise innovative solutions and take initiative. This empowerment boosts job satisfaction and motivation while enhancing project results. Empowerment fosters a proactive and dynamic work environment where employees feel appreciated and inspired to give their best.

Integrating these humanistic values into leadership practices can profoundly transform organizational culture and effectiveness. Leaders create a work environment where employees feel valued, understood, and motivated by demonstrating empathy, integrity, respect, compassion, fairness, authenticity, and empowerment. These values enhance individual and team performance and contribute to sustainable organizational success. The significance of these values lies in their power to turn the workplace into a thriving ecosystem where innovation, productivity, and employee satisfaction coexist and reinforce each other, inspiring managers to embrace these values and drive positive change.

Overcoming Challenges in Upholding Humanistic Values

It can be challenging for most managers to uphold humanistic values in corporate life. The pressures and demands of the business environment often prioritize efficiency, profitability, and short-term results over the well-being and development of employees. Managers are frequently under intense pressure to meet performance targets and deliver quick outcomes, which can lead to a focus on metrics and deliverables at the expense of human considerations. Hierarchical structures and competitive atmospheres can create environments where vulnerability and empathy are seen as weaknesses. The constant need to prove one's competence and authority can make it difficult for managers to embrace values such as compassion, fairness, and authenticity. Recognizing these challenges is the first step toward overcoming them and creating a more humanistic workplace.

Another major obstacle is the insufficient support and training in humanistic leadership practices. Many managers lack the skills to effectively incorporate these values into their daily management styles. Traditional management education and corporate training programs often focus on technical skills and strategic thinking while overlooking the interpersonal and emotional intelligence aspects of leadership.

It's also important to acknowledge that systemic issues such as bias, discrimination, and inequality within organizations can hinder efforts to uphold humanistic values. These issues can make it difficult for well-meaning managers to act on their principles. Despite these challenges, it is crucial for managers to understand the long-term benefits of creating a supportive and empathetic workplace. They should actively seek opportunities for personal and professional development that align with these values. By advocating for support and training, managers can feel empowered and better prepared to incorporate these values into their leadership practices.

Ultimately, overcoming these challenges requires a commitment to continuous learning and growth. Managers must cultivate self-awareness, seek feedback from peers and mentors, and remain open to new approaches. By doing so, they can foster a work environment where empathy, trust, and respect are not just ideals but everyday practices that drive sustainable success and positive impact.

Human-Centered Leadership: Insights from Psychology

Humanistic values in management, which are based on the theories of Abraham Maslow and Carl Rogers, emphasize respect, autonomy, and individual development within the organization. Unlike traditional management approaches that prioritize efficiency and output, humanistic management aims to understand and nurture the intrinsic motivations of each employee. By focusing on human dignity and personal growth, this approach aims to create a more fulfilling and productive work environment. Embracing humanistic values in management reflects a broader shift in organizational culture that places a higher value on employee well-being, satisfaction, and development, ultimately leading to increased productivity and employee loyalty. Integrating Rogers's and Maslow's theories into management practices underscores a shift towards more empathetic and growth-oriented leadership styles. These psychologists, pivotal in the humanistic psychology movement, provide frameworks that prioritize individual well-being and growth—crucial elements for organizational success.

Abraham Maslow's impact on humanistic psychology, particularly in leadership, is profound, notably through his hierarchy of needs theory. This model, starting with basic physical necessities like food and shelter and progressing to safety, love and belonging, esteem, and self-actualization, offers a practical roadmap for understanding employee motivations. In a leadership context, this means recognizing that employees are not solely driven by financial rewards but also by the need for safety, belonging, and personal growth. By creating an environment that supports these diverse needs, leaders can unlock unprecedented levels of motivation and productivity among their teams, instilling a sense of confidence in their leadership approach.

Similarly, Carl Rogers has made significant contributions to humanistic psychology that echo present-day leadership practices. Rogers championed the principles of empathy, unconditional positive regard, and congruence, emphasizing the importance of a supportive and non-judgmental environment for individual growth. He believed that for people to realize their potential fully, they must be in conditions that provide them with genuineness, acceptance, and empathy. These principles are increasingly applied in leadership strategies, advocating for a supportive work atmosphere where employees feel valued and understood. Rogers's concepts have laid the groundwork for creating an organizational culture where employees are motivated not by fear or obligation but by an intrinsic desire to grow and contribute to their community, adding to an optimistic outlook on workplace culture.

Integrating the ideas of Rogers and Maslow into leadership and management practices requires a strategic shift towards more people-centered policies and a culture that emphasizes individual growth within the framework of organizational objectives. Leaders who understand and apply Maslow's hierarchy of needs recognize the complex nature of their team members' motivations and strive to create an environment where those needs can be met. This approach goes beyond the traditional focus on salary and job security to encompass emotional and psychological well-being, personal development, and a sense of belonging and appreciation. Similarly, applying Carl Rogers's principles involves establishing a leadership style that is empathetic, transparent, and encourages open communication. By providing unconditional positive regard, leaders can create a safe space for innovation, candid feedback, and personal development. This leads to higher job satisfaction and morale and builds a strong foundation for resilience and adaptability within the team.

These concepts align closely with the current emphasis on "psychological safety" and "flow psychology." Psychological safety, popularized by research from Harvard professor Amy Edmondson, refers to an environment where employees feel safe to take risks, express their ideas, and make mistakes without fear of judgment or retribution. This directly relates to Rogers's principles of empathy and unconditional positive regard, creating a workplace where individuals can thrive. Flow psychology, introduced by Mihály Csíkszentmihályi, describes a state of deep engagement and productivity achieved when individuals are challenged and supported appropriately.[66] By understanding and addressing Maslow's hierarchy of needs, managers can help create conditions conducive to flow, thus strengthening higher levels of motivation and performance.

Leaders can embody these humanistic values by actively listening to their employees, acknowledging their achievements, encouraging professional development, and facilitating a work environment that supports both team and individual successes. This holistic course of action for leadership and management enriches the workplace culture and boosts productivity, innovation, and loyalty, achieving the people dividend.

The Evolution of Humanistic Management and the Emergence of the People Dividend

Incorporating humanistic values into management traces back to the human relations movement and the subsequent development of organizational behavior as a field of study. These disciplines emphasized the importance of psychological well-being in the workplace and its impact on productivity. Humanistic management practices have evolved significantly since their inception, thanks to the contributions of critical thinkers like Abraham Maslow and Carl Rogers.

Business leaders and executives keen on driving employee satisfaction and business success find the concept of the people dividend particularly persuasive. By recognizing the economic value derived from investing in their employees' well-being and development, they can cultivate a positive work environment and enhance organizational performance. This aligns well with the strategic goals of leadership, making it easier to gain buy-in for people-centered initiatives.

Similarly, human resources (HR) professionals dedicated to talent management, employee engagement, and organization development can leverage the people dividend to enhance their strategies. By integrating these principles, HR can support organizational goals more effectively, ensuring that employees are not just managed but critical drivers of value creation within the company. This approach helps build a more motivated, resourceful, and loyal workforce, contributing significantly to overall business success.

When an employee transitions from a team practicing humanistic management to one adhering to machine-like practices, the shift can be jarring and significantly impact their overall well-being and performance. In a humanistic environment, the individual likely enjoyed autonomy, a sense of belonging, and opportunities for personal and professional growth, all contributing to higher job satisfaction and engagement. Such a setting encourages open communication, empathy, and a supportive culture that values the individual's contributions and personal development. Moving to a mechanistic team, the focus shifts sharply to efficiency, standardization, and the bottom line, often at the expense of individual employee needs, creativity, and personal expression. The abrupt change can lead to alienation, decreased motivation, and decreased job satisfaction as the employee struggles to adjust to a more impersonal, less flexible working environment.

Furthermore, the transition to a machine-like management style can also stunt an employee's growth and innovation capabilities. In humanistic settings, the emphasis on individual strengths and creativity promotes innovation and a proactive approach to problem-solving. Employees are encouraged to take risks, think outside the box, and contribute their unique perspectives. However, in a mechanistic framework, the rigidity and the focus on standardization suppress these tendencies. The employee, once thriving in an environment that celebrated diversity of thought and innovation, may find themselves confined by rigid procedures and discouraged from expressing unconventional ideas. This hampers their personal and professional development and can negatively affect the team and organization's capacity to adapt and evolve, thereby impacting the organization's long-term success and sustainability.

The concept of the people dividend evolves these humanistic principles, adapting them to present organizational challenges and opportunities. Unlike traditional humanistic management, the people dividend explicitly recognizes the economic value of investing in employees' well-being and development. It builds on Maslow's and Rogers's insights but goes further by quantifying the returns on investments in people-centered practices. This system provides a compelling business case for adopting such practices, making it easier to gain buy-in from stakeholders focused on financial performance.

The people dividend is particularly relevant in the current knowledge-based economy, where creativity, innovation, and adaptability are crucial for success. Organizations that invest in their employees' development and well-being can unlock higher engagement, loyalty, and productivity levels. This, in turn, leads to better business outcomes, including increased profitability, market share, and long-term sustainability. By viewing employees as resources to be managed and critical drivers of value creation, the people dividend shifts the focus from short-term efficiency gains to long-term strategic growth.

Moreover, the people dividend emphasizes the importance of creating an inclusive and diverse work environment. Diversity of thought and experience is a powerful driver of innovation and problem-solving. Organizations can better navigate complex challenges and seize new opportunities by establishing an environment where all employees feel valued and empowered to contribute their unique perspectives. This inclusive plan aligns with the broader public push for equity and social responsibility, enhancing the organization's reputation and appeal to top talent.

As we move forward, the people dividend offers a new chapter in the history of management. It builds on the foundational ideas of Maslow and Rogers but adapts them to contemporary organizational realities. By integrating humanistic values with a clear focus on economic outcomes, the people dividend represents an advancement in management practices that promises to drive employee satisfaction and business success.

Advocating for People-Centered Leadership: Strategies for Success

Integrating humanistic values can significantly enhance your workplace. This process not only benefits individual employees but also drives organizational success. However, advocating for such a shift requires strategic efforts to persuade peers, your team, and management.

While the term "humanistic values" might resonate deeply with some, it can sound abstract or even off-putting in a corporate environment. A more palatable and relatable term could be "people-centered leadership." This concept emphasizes putting people first, recognizing their unique contributions, engendering a supportive environment, and prioritizing their growth and well-being. By framing it as people-centered leadership, you can make the principles more accessible and appealing to a broader audience within your organization.

The CEO would be particularly interested in people-centered leadership because it directly correlates with increased employee engagement, productivity, and innovation. A people-centered plan cultivates a loyal and motivated workforce, leading to lower turnover rates and higher performance levels. Consequently, this translates into achieving business goals more efficiently and creating a competitive edge in the market.

Sticking your neck out for people-centered leadership is about advocating for a better, more effective way to lead. It means committing to a vision where employees feel valued and supported, unlocking their full potential. This commitment demonstrates your belief in a leadership style that enhances the work environment and drives long-term success for the organization.

Moreover, by championing people-centered leadership, you position yourself as a forward-thinking leader dedicated to improving the workplace. This can elevate your professional reputation, open up new opportunities for career advancement, and contribute to personal fulfillment as you witness the positive impacts of your efforts. Embracing these values allows you to leave a lasting legacy of meaningful change within your organization.

Here are ten actionable strategies to effectively promote and integrate people-centered leadership within your organization:

1. Craft an Irresistible Narrative

Begin by telling a story that resonates. Share real-life examples or case studies of people-centered leadership that have improved employee engagement and organizational success. This helps create an emotional connection and vividly illustrates the potential benefits.

2. Engage Key Stakeholders Early

Identify key stakeholders and involve them early in the process. Create a coalition of supporters who understand and are committed to promoting people-centered values. Their influence can be instrumental in driving cultural change across different levels of the organization.

3. Present Data-Driven Insights

Use data and research to support your case. Present metrics showing how people-centered practices correlate with higher employee satisfaction, lower turnover rates, and improved productivity. Concrete data can be a powerful tool to convince skeptics and demonstrate the value of this system.

4. Pilot People-Centered Initiatives

Implement small-scale pilot programs to showcase the impact of people-centered leadership. For example, initiate a mentorship program or a diversity and inclusion task force. Use the outcomes of these pilots to build a strong argument for broader adoption.

5. Facilitate Workshops and Training

Organize workshops and training sessions focused on people-centered leadership principles. Equip leaders and managers with the skills and knowledge to develop and sustain empathy, inclusivity, and personal growth within their teams. Empower them to become champions of these values.

6. Create Interactive Platforms for Dialogue

Establish forums, town halls, or online platforms where

employees can voice their opinions, share ideas, and provide feedback. This promotes open communication and reinforces the importance of considering diverse perspectives in decision-making processes. Encouraging dialogue helps build trust and transparency within the team.

7. Utilize Internal Communication Channels

Leverage internal communication channels to consistently share success stories, testimonials, and updates related to people-centered initiatives. Regularly highlighting these efforts keeps the conversation alive and demonstrates an ongoing commitment from leadership. Consistent communication helps maintain momentum and enthusiasm for these initiatives.

8. Recognize and Reward People-Centered Behaviors

Develop recognition programs that celebrate employees and leaders who exemplify people-centered values. Publicly acknowledging these behaviors reinforces their importance and encourages others to follow suit. Recognition can also boost morale and motivate further positive behavior.

9. Integrate People-Centered Values into Policies

Review and revise company policies to reflect people-centered principles. Ensure that performance reviews, recruitment processes, and career development plans are aligned with the values of respect, fairness, and personal growth. This alignment shows a genuine commitment to embedding these values in the organizational fabric.

10. *Lead by Example*

Consistently demonstrate the people-centered values you advocate. Show empathy, integrity, and concern for employee well-being in your actions and decisions. Your behavior sets a powerful precedent and inspires others to adopt similar values.

By implementing these strategies, you can effectively advocate for and embed people-centered values within your corporate culture. The journey may require persistence and patience, but the rewards are worthwhile. Not only will you see an enhancement in individual employee experiences, but you will also witness a more resilient, enterprising, and high-performing organization.

In conclusion, integrating people-centered values into your leadership framework is a moral imperative and a strategic advantage. Leading an environment that prioritizes respect, autonomy, diversity, and personal growth, you unlock your teams' full potential. This leads to the people dividend—an increase in engagement, innovation, and performance that propels your organization towards sustained success.

Examining the Limitations of the People Dividend

Despite the many benefits of leveraging the people dividend, it is not without limitations and may not always be beneficial or practical in certain business contexts. One significant limitation is the potential for reduced operational efficiency. The emphasis on individual contributions and personal development can sometimes lead to a lack of standardized procedures, making it challenging to achieve high levels of efficiency and consistency across an organization. In industries where precision and standardization are critical to success, such as manufacturing or high-volume retail, a people dividend formula may inadvertently lead to disruptions in workflow and decreased productivity.

Another challenge with focusing on the people dividend lies in its scalability. While small to medium-sized organizations may find it easier to implement such values due to their closer-knit teams and simpler organizational structures, larger corporations might struggle. However, with the right strategies and adaptations, the potential for growth and development in a vast workforce with diverse needs and preferences can be harnessed. The individual attention and investment that form the core of the people dividend can be maintained as the organization grows, ensuring employees feel valued and upholding the very principles the system aims to uphold.

Furthermore, a heavy reliance on the people dividend can lead to difficulties in decision-making and conflict resolution. However, with a strong emphasis on clear communication and alignment of personal development and employee empowerment with organizational goals, these challenges can be effectively managed. In situations where tough decisions need to be made, such as downsizing or reallocating resources away from underperforming departments, a strong focus on maintaining positive relationships and ensuring employee satisfaction can be balanced with necessary actions, ensuring the organization's long-term viability.

The success of the people dividend also heavily depends on the competencies and values of the leaders implementing it. Not all managers have the emotional intelligence, empathy, and communication skills required to lead effectively with a people-focused formula. Without these crucial skills, attempts at leveraging the people dividend may fall flat, leading to skepticism and cynicism among employees. This inconsistency in leadership capabilities can create an environment where the principles of a people-centered process are inconsistently applied, eroding trust and diminishing the potential benefits.

Moreover, the people dividend practice might face resistance from stakeholders focused on short-term financial performance. It's important to acknowledge that investors and board members often prioritize measurable outcomes like profit margins and market share over qualitative aspects like employee satisfaction and development. This misalignment can create tension and pressure to revert to more traditional management practices, particularly during times of economic uncertainty or poor financial performance. Recognizing these concerns and finding ways to address them can help successfully implement the people dividend framework.

In addition, implementing a people dividend strategy requires significant time and resource investment. Training programs, employee development initiatives, and systematic feedback systems demand financial and human capital. For organizations operating on tight budgets or within highly competitive markets, allocating resources to these areas can be challenging, potentially limiting the extent to which they can fully embrace this way of being and doing.

While the people dividend offers numerous advantages in delivering a positive work environment, its application may not be universally beneficial or practical. Understanding the context in which this process can thrive is vital to leveraging its benefits while mitigating potential drawbacks. As Nelson Mandela once said, "Action without vision is only passing time, vision without action is merely daydreaming, but vision with action can change the world." This quote underscores the importance of not just having a people-centered strategy (vision) but also implementing it effectively (action). It highlights that the people dividend requires both strategic foresight and diligent execution to make a meaningful impact.

Extending People-Centered Management Beyond Organizational Boundaries

Leaders can implement people-centered management through various practices that extend beyond the confines of their organization. By engaging with external communities and talent pools, organizations can showcase their commitment to humanistic values. This course of action helps attract top talent and cultivates a positive reputation, aligning the organization's actions with its core values.

Such outward-facing initiatives are essential in

demonstrating that people-centered values are not limited to internal operations but are integral to the organization's philosophy. Engaging with the broader community provides opportunities to make a meaningful impact while reinforcing the importance of respect, empathy, and personal growth in all interactions. Below are eight effective strategies to demonstrate people-centered management externally.

1. Community Engagement Programs

Establish programs that encourage employees to volunteer in local communities. Partner with non-profit organizations to support education, health, and environmental initiatives. This benefits the community and highlights the organization's commitment to social responsibility.

2. Inclusive Hiring Practices

Develop recruitment strategies that actively seek out diverse candidates from various backgrounds. Attend job fairs in underserved areas, collaborate with minority-focused professional networks, and create internship opportunities for underrepresented groups.

3. Educational Partnerships

Partner with local schools, colleges, and universities to offer mentorship programs, internships, and scholarships. Providing educational support demonstrates a commitment to developing future talent and strengthens the organization's presence in the community.

4. Public Recognition Programs

Sponsor or create awards and recognition programs that celebrate achievements in the broader community. Acknowledge leaders, innovators, and community activists who align with the organization's values, reinforcing the importance of people-centered leadership.

5. Open Forums and Workshops

Host public forums, workshops, and seminars on topics related to leadership, personal development, and industry trends. These events provide valuable learning opportunities for the community and position the organization as a thought leader dedicated to growth and development.

6. Corporate Social Responsibility (CSR) Initiatives

Launch CSR projects that address pressing societal issues such as sustainability, social justice, or public health. Engage employees in these initiatives and communicate the impact to the broader community, demonstrating a genuine commitment to making a difference.

7. Talent Development Programs

Create talent development programs that offer training and skill-building opportunities to individuals outside the organization. Partner with community centers, vocational schools, and local businesses to provide resources and support for career advancement.

8. *Employee Ambassadors*

Encourage employees to act as ambassadors for the organization by participating in community events, speaking engagements, and professional associations. Their involvement can help build strong community ties and showcase the organization's dedication to people-centered values.

Implementing these external-facing strategies can help demonstrate your organization's commitment to people-centered management. By actively engaging with communities and talent pools, you can attract top talent, enhance your brand reputation, and make a meaningful impact beyond your organizational boundaries.

Conclusion

The exploration of humanistic values within leadership and management underscores their profound impact on organizational success and employee well-being. Humanistic values such as empathy, respect, and personal growth cultivate a supportive and collaborative environment. Leaders who embody these values promote trust and morale and drive overall team effectiveness. This mode is vividly illustrated when managers take the time to understand and address their employees' personal challenges, thereby enhancing both individual and collective performance.

As we consider Maslow's and Rogers's theories, it becomes clear that their insights are foundational to human-centered leadership. Maslow's hierarchy of needs and Rogers's emphasis on empathy and personal growth provide a robust framework for understanding and nurturing employees' intrinsic motivations. Organizations prioritizing these humanistic principles create work environments where employees feel valued and motivated to reach their full potential. This focus on employee development marks a significant departure from traditional management practices that prioritize efficiency over individual well-being.

The evolution of humanistic management has led to the emergence of the people dividend, a concept that recognizes the economic value of investing in employees' well-being and development. The people dividend builds on the principles of Maslow and Rogers, offering a forceful business case for adopting people-centered practices. By quantifying the returns on such investments, this framework aligns humanistic values with organizational goals, ensuring that employee satisfaction and business success go hand in hand. This paradigm shift highlights the importance of viewing employees as resources and critical drivers of value creation.

Advocating for people-centered leadership requires strategic communication and a nuanced understanding of organizational dynamics. By framing humanistic values as "people-centered leadership," advocates can present these ideas in a more relatable and actionable manner. This pathway benefits individual employees and enhances overall organizational performance. Effective advocacy involves demonstrating the tangible benefits of people-centered practices, such as increased engagement, innovation, and loyalty, thereby contributing to long-term business success.

Despite its many advantages, the people dividend methodology is not without limitations. In specific contexts, such as industries that demand high levels of standardization and operational efficiency, the emphasis on individual development may lead to challenges. Organizations must carefully balance humanistic values with the need for consistency and precision in their workflows. Recognizing these limitations is crucial for developing a balanced and pragmatic practice of people-centered management.

Extending people-centered management beyond an organization's confines demonstrates a commitment to humanistic values on a broader scale. Engaging with external communities and talent pools showcases an organization's dedication to these principles, reinforcing its reputation and furthering goodwill. By implementing strategies that promote people-centered values externally, organizations can build a strong, inclusive brand that resonates with stakeholders and attracts top talent, thereby driving sustainable success.

In conclusion, incorporating humanistic values into management practices significantly enhances contemporary leadership. By prioritizing empathy, personal growth, and employee well-being, leaders can cultivate more fulfilling and productive work environments. The people dividend presents a robust framework for aligning these humanistic principles with organizational goals, guaranteeing that investing in people yields substantial returns. As organizations progress, adopting people-centered leadership will be crucial for achieving long-term success and upholding a culture of care and innovation.

Reflection Questions for Chapter Seven

- How do humanistic values such as empathy, respect, and personal growth contribute to a supportive and collaborative work environment?

- In what ways can managers effectively address their employees' personal challenges to enhance overall team effectiveness?

- How do Maslow's hierarchy of needs and Rogers's emphasis on empathy and personal growth provide a foundation for human-centered leadership?

- How does the concept of the people dividend align humanistic values with organizational goals, and what are the tangible benefits of this alignment?

- What are the key differences between traditional management practices and those that prioritize employee development?

Chapter 8:

The Future of Work with The People Dividend

Capturing the attention of business leaders and scholars alike, the concept of humanistic management has been gaining momentum, particularly over the last decade. As we've explored, this approach prioritizes the well-being and development of employees just as much as profitability and efficiency. It's not merely a trend but a fundamental shift in how we conceptualize business operations. At its core, humanistic management holds that businesses should serve the broader community, contributing positively to the world while fostering a workplace environment that promotes dignity, respect, and growth opportunities for all its members.

The transition towards humanistic management principles is a direct response to the growing recognition of the unsustainable nature of traditional business practices, which often prioritize short-term gains over long-term resilience and human values. The emphasis on metrics and outputs has frequently led to neglecting the human element—the core that drives innovation, commitment, and performance. By recentering the focus on people, businesses are rediscovering the immense value of trust, self-esteem, and engagement in driving sustainable success.

However, this shift is not without its challenges. Implementing humanistic management practices requires a profound transformation in corporate culture, leadership styles, and operational strategies. It demands openness, flexibility, and commitment beyond conventional management paradigms. Leaders must become champions of empathy, inclusivity, and environmental responsibility, encouraging a culture where feedback is welcomed and failures are viewed as opportunities for learning and growth.

The impact of a humanistic management system is significant. It offers employees a work environment that respects their individuality, goals, and need for work-life balance, resulting in increased satisfaction and engagement. For organizations, it means having a more motivated and productive workforce that can drive innovation and maintain competitiveness. Additionally, for society, businesses that operate under humanistic principles make positive contributions to social and environmental well-being, establishing new standards for corporate responsibility.

Yet, the future of work with humanistic management is not predetermined. It is shaped by the choices of today's leaders and the collective will of all stakeholders involved. To fully realize its potential, a concerted effort is required to redefine success, not just in terms of finance but quality of life, social impact, and ecological sustainability. This entails developing new metrics for assessing performance, embedding a leadership mindset that values emotional intelligence as highly as business acumen, and embedding humanistic values into every aspect of organizational operation.

The role of technology in the future is incredibly important. Digital tools and platforms provide great opportunities for improving workplace flexibility and learning. When used carefully, technology can support people-centered management, allowing for remote work and creating a sense of community and connection among teams that are dispersed and distant. However, it also presents new considerations and challenges that need to be approached thoughtfully to ensure that technology improves human interaction and well-being rather than detracting from it.

The concept of humanistic management offers an optimistic perspective on the future of work, outlining the ideals that businesses should strive for in the twenty-first century. It emphasizes the need for leaders to pursue a balanced approach that integrates profit and purpose, efficiency and empathy, and innovation and integrity. This approach is seen as raising the success of businesses while contributing to a fair and thriving global community.

The Workplace of Tomorrow

Looking ahead, we can foresee a significant workplace transformation beyond physical spaces and traditional schedules. This change will be focused on creating work cultures that prioritize people. For example, the U.S. is testing a four-day workweek to improve employee well-being. A bill introduced by Senator Bernie Sanders in March 2024 highlights the growing support for this model.[67]Technology is also set to change, from tying workers to their desks to freeing them up, encouraging a more creative and productive work environment.

The concept of a four-day workweek, a departure from traditional work models, offers a multitude of benefits for both employees and employers. A comprehensive study conducted in Iceland from 2015 to 2019, involving over 2,500 workers, revealed that reducing work hours without reducing pay leads to a significant decrease in stress levels, a boost in job satisfaction, and maintained or even improved productivity.[68] This underscores the fact that adjusting work hours can foster a healthier, happier workforce, which in turn translates into better business outcomes.

Moreover, the rise of remote workforces is revolutionizing how organizations function. The shift in 2020, propelled by the global pandemic, demonstrated that many roles can be effectively performed outside the confines of a traditional office. According to a Gallup poll, even after the initial phase of the pandemic, 45% of U.S. full-time employees were working from home either partially or fully.[69] Remote work is not just a change in location; it's a shift towards using digital tools to foster more inclusive company cultures, where everyone feels valued and included.

These new workplace trends also positively impact the environment. For instance, remote work has drastically reduced daily commuting, reducing carbon emissions. Global Workplace Analytics estimates that if those with remote-capable jobs worked from home half the time, it would be like removing ten million cars from the road annually.[70]

As workplaces evolve, ensuring digital equality is crucial. Access to reliable high-speed internet and modern technology is essential for everyone to participate in the future workforce. The digital divide poses a big challenge, especially in rural and underserved areas. This highlights the urgent need for investment in infrastructure and education to close this gap and offer equal opportunities for all.

Digital transformation is not just changing the workplace, it's expanding horizons. It's opening doors to a global talent pool where small and large companies can tap into diverse skills and perspectives. This shift often necessitates the use of digital tools to keep teams connected and enable seamless collaboration across time zones. However, it also presents challenges, such as managing cultural differences, ensuring effective communication across languages, and navigating various legal requirements. Yet, with careful planning and ongoing efforts, this can lead to a more productive work environment, one that's centered around people and their growth.

Employee health and wellness are becoming increasingly vital to an organization's success. Including wellness programs, mental health support, and ergonomic work environments in company policies shows an understanding that employee well-being significantly affects productivity and creativity. These initiatives are becoming attractive features for companies wanting to attract and retain top talent.

Leadership styles are also changing, with more emphasis placed on emotional intelligence. Future leaders will inspire and engage their teams, promoting a culture of openness and innovation. Being adaptable and open to feedback is becoming more valued than autocratic decision-making. This shift towards empathetic leadership highlights the importance of nurturing a positive work culture and supporting employee growth. In turn, this can lead to increased job satisfaction and retention rates for companies.

The future workplace is poised to embrace changes like the four-day workweek and the rise of remote work teams. These developments signal a move towards more adaptable and employee-centric work environments. While challenges such as digital equity and maintaining corporate culture remotely remain, it is evident that the workplace is evolving to prioritize the well-being of both the planet and its people.

Crafting a People-Centered Workplace

Crafting a people-centered workplace is essential for harnessing human potential. The first step is to prioritize employee health by providing comprehensive health benefits and implementing wellness programs. This also means designing workspaces that promote positive interactions and personal comfort. For instance, using ergonomic office furniture, creating meditation or quiet reflection areas, and incorporating opportunities for physical activity throughout the workday can significantly boost employee satisfaction and productivity.

Another critical component is empowering employees through flexible work arrangements. By allowing team members to have a say in their schedules, work locations, and even some aspects of their job roles, companies can improve engagement, reduce turnover, and attract top talent. Flexible working conditions demonstrate trust and respect for the individual needs of employees, leading to a more motivated and committed workforce.

Investing in learning and professional development is paramount in a people-centered workplace. The rapid pace of technological change requires a workforce that can evolve and adapt. Offering training programs, workshops, and courses helps employees enhance their current skills and prepares them for future challenges and career advancement opportunities.

A diverse workforce brings diverse perspectives, experiences, and ideas, driving innovation and better decision-making. Implementing policies promoting diversity, equity, inclusion, and belonging (DEIB), from recruitment practices to career advancement opportunities, establishes a workplace where everyone feels valued and heard.

Communication and transparency are the bedrock of a people-centered workplace. Establishing open lines of communication where feedback is encouraged, actively sought, and valued facilitates a culture of trust and mutual respect. Regular updates about company performance, policy changes, and general news help employees feel connected and integral to the organization's mission.

In the long run, crafting a people-centered workplace aims to create an environment where employees can thrive, feel valued, and are motivated to contribute their best work towards the organization's goals. This strategy recognizes the extensive nature of employee well-being and its critical impact on productivity, innovation, and competitive advantage. By putting the well-being of employees at the forefront, businesses cultivate a resilient, adaptable, and driven workforce prepared to meet the challenges of the future.

Rethinking Human Resources (HR) Systems and Approaches

Rethinking HR systems and methods is a crucial step in building a more adaptable and innovative organization. Traditional HR practices often prioritize administrative efficiency over strategic value, focus on compliance rather than engagement, and regard employees more as resources than as integral stakeholders in the organization's success. A future-focused lens to HR emphasizes developing talent, enhancing engagement, and supporting a culture that aligns with the organization's goals and values. This requires a shift from a policy-driven to a people-centered HR paradigm.

The recruitment and onboarding process is one of the first

areas to address in transforming HR systems. In the hyper-competitive talent market, organizations must move beyond simply filling positions to strategically attracting individuals who are not just qualified but also aligned with the company's culture and long-term objectives. This involves leveraging data analytics for smarter hiring decisions and ensuring new hires feel connected and valued from day one. Adopting technology platforms that facilitate seamless communication and integration into the team can significantly enhance the onboarding process.

Performance management is another domain ripe for innovation. The traditional annual review process is increasingly seen as outdated, with forward-thinking companies adopting routine feedback systems that encourage consistent dialogue between managers and employees. Such a pathway helps identify growth opportunities, address concerns in in a timely manner, and promote a culture of sustained improvement. By leveraging technology, companies can implement platforms that facilitate regular goal setting and recognition, making the performance management process more dynamic and engaging.

It is crucial to prioritize employee learning and development as a central component of an updated HR strategy. In today's fast-paced environment, we need a workforce that is agile and committed to continuous learning. Providing customized learning paths, promoting cross-functional projects, and offering access to mentorship and coaching can support employees in their career growth and progression. By investing in digital learning platforms, we can offer flexibility and accessibility, empowering employees to improve their skills in line with their personal and organizational objectives.

The concept of employee wellness has expanded significantly, moving beyond physical health to encompass mental and emotional well-being. Modern HR practices acknowledge the significance of supporting employees holistically. This can involve initiatives like flexible working options, mental health support programs, and policies that promote work-life balance. Establishing an environment where employees feel supported in all aspects of their well-being is crucial.

Diversity, equity, inclusion, and belonging must be woven into the fabric of organizational practices, beyond rhetoric to genuine action. This involves analyzing and redesigning HR processes to eliminate bias, ensure equity in pay and promotion opportunities, and deliver a culture where diverse perspectives are respected and valued. Training and awareness programs can help build understanding and empathy, but real change requires commitment at all levels of the organization, especially from leadership.

Finally, the role of HR technology must be balanced in modernizing HR systems, plans, and methods. While technology offers tools that streamline processes and provide actionable insights, from recruitment and onboarding to performance management and employee engagement, it's important to remember that technology should be seen as a facilitator rather than a replacement for human interaction. The goal of rethinking HR systems is to create a more human-centered workplace where technology supports and enhances the employee experience, but not at the cost of diminishing the importance of human interaction. By innovating HR systems, organizations can better align their people practices with the needs of a rapidly changing world. This improves the employee experience and drives organizational success, creating a workplace that is adaptable, engaging, and ready for the future.

The Imperative for Business Leaders

The imperative for business leaders today goes beyond traditional management practices; it demands a commitment to leading with foresight and a genuine investment in the well-being of their employees. Leaders prioritizing a human-centered system are better poised to motivate and drive innovation within their teams. This leadership archetype recognizes that people are not merely resources but the core asset that propels the organization forward. By embodying values promoting respect and dignity, leaders create an environment where every individual feels valued and empowered to contribute their best.

Furthermore, business leaders must be adept at navigating the complexities of a global market characterized by technological advancements and shifting economic conditions. This requires a strategic mindset and the agility to adapt to change head-on. Leaders must, therefore, cultivate a forward-looking vision, anchoring their strategies in sustainability. This vision must be communicated clearly and consistently, ensuring that all team members are aligned with the organization's goals. By understanding their crucial role in achieving these goals, team members feel appreciated and motivated, contributing to the organization's success.

Equally crucial is developing leadership competencies that enable effective decision-making amid ambiguity. This involves guiding a culture where critical thinking and informed risk-taking are valued and encouraged. Leaders must champion a learning-oriented mindset, where mistakes are not just tolerated but viewed as valuable learning opportunities for growth and experimentation. By doing so, they can build resilient, adaptable, and equipped teams to tackle tomorrow's challenges, thereby reassuring their audience and reducing their fear of failure.

In addition, sustainability and corporate social responsibility are paramount. Business leaders are central to ensuring that their organizations operate profitably and ethically. This encompasses various practices, from environmental stewardship to ethical labor practices and community engagement. Leaders can build trust and credibility by integrating these principles into the core business strategy. This commitment to ethical leadership enhances the organization's reputation and contributes to a more sustainable and equitable global economy.

Finally, in this digital transformation era, leaders must harness the power of technology to drive efficiency and innovation. However, technological advancements must be balanced with a human touch. Leaders should leverage digital tools to enhance the employee experience, from facilitating remote work to offering personalized learning opportunities. Yet, the focus should always remain on championing meaningful connections and ensuring that technology serves to augment rather than replace human interaction. In demonstrating a commitment to both technological progress and the human element of leadership, business leaders can create a successful organization that is also a great place to work.

Examples of Humanistic Values in Practice

Numerous examples demonstrate the practical application of humanistic values in management, spanning from small local enterprises to large multinational corporations. These instances showcase the positive outcomes that can arise from prioritizing the well-being and individuality of employees, not only in terms of fostering high levels of job satisfaction but also in driving superior overall organizational success.

Employees' responses to the practice of humanistic management manifest in various positive ways, significantly impacting their level of engagement and overall satisfaction at work. Employees feel genuinely appreciated when leaders focus on treating individuals with respect, recognizing their contributions, and valuing their well-being. This appreciation showcases a deeper emotional connection to their work and the organization, a crucial element of engagement. Employees who feel valued are more likely to go above and beyond, contributing to a culture of excellence.

The practice of humanistic management also leads to increased job satisfaction among employees. By creating an environment that prioritizes personal growth and meaningful work, humanistic leadership addresses the intrinsic motivations of employees. When individuals find purpose in their work and see opportunities for development, their satisfaction levels rise. This, in turn, leads to higher engagement levels, as satisfied employees are more committed to their organization's goals and more inclined to put in discretionary effort.

Another response to humanistic management is enhanced trust in leadership. Humanistic values like transparency, integrity, and fairness lay the foundation for trust. Employees who believe their leaders have their best interests at heart are more likely to trust them. This trust is critical for engagement; it enables open communication and encourages feedback, both precursors for creating a sense of security. When employees trust their leaders, they feel more supported and empowered to take on challenges and contribute ideas, further deepening their engagement.

Humanistic management practices also contribute to a stronger sense of belonging among employees. Inclusive leadership strategies that celebrate diversity and encourage belonging make individuals feel like they are part of a community. Feeling connected to one's colleagues and the organization enhances emotional engagement, which is the emotional commitment the employee has to the organization and its goals. This sense of belonging can act as a buffer against stress and burnout, leading to better team performance.

Lastly, the practice of humanistic management dramatically improves communication within the organization. By valuing each employee's voice, leaders can break down silos and facilitate effective collaboration. Improved communication enhances understanding and alignment on goals, enabling employees to see how their work contributes to the larger mission. This awareness is directly linked to increased engagement, as employees who understand their impact are more motivated and committed to delivering their best work. Overall, implementing humanistic values in management improves individual well-being and leads to a more dedicated workforce.

Conclusion

As workplace dynamics continue to evolve, the principles underlying the people dividend will remain central to creating organizations where employees do their best work. Leaders and organizations that prioritize these tenets will not only excel in adapting to the new norms but will also play a central role in shaping the future of work. Businesses need to recognize that the integration of these elements into their core strategy is beneficial and critical for sustainable growth and success in the long term. In an environment where innovation is balanced with inclusivity and technological progress goes hand in hand with personal development, companies can ensure that they are prepared for the challenges and opportunities that lie ahead.

The emphasis on learning and development, alongside a commitment to DEIB, is more than just a trend; it reflects the changing expectations of the workforce. Organizations that adapt to these expectations and incorporate them into their operational and strategic efforts showcase their resilience and dedication to being forward-thinking in their approach to business and employee engagement. Companies like those described in various places throughout the book exemplify what it means to build a culture that sets a high bar for others to follow.

Furthermore, while technology presents challenges such as digital overload and the potential for reduced human interaction, it can also be a powerful tool for improving productivity, collaboration, and employee satisfaction. The key lies in finding the right balance that augments human capabilities and strengthens connections rather than diminishing them. Organizations that succeed in this will lead the way in creating work environments that are more likely to produce dividends through people.

In conclusion, as we look to the future, the path to success for any organization lies in its ability to adapt and grow in these critical areas. By maintaining a focus on the human aspect of the workplace, companies can thrive amidst today's complexities. This comprehensive plan will enhance their competitive edge and contribute to a more equitable and prosperous world. The way forward requires a shared effort rooted in a united vision for a better future of work where everyone can succeed and contribute to their fullest potential.

Reflection Questions for Chapter Eight

- How does your organization currently support learning and development for its employees? Are there areas for improvement?

- What initiatives can your organization implement to enhance people-centered performance and maximize the people dividend by investing in employee well-being and development?

- How can leaders in your organization better exemplify ethical leadership? What specific actions can they take to prioritize human-centered practices?

- In what ways can your organization ensure that inclusivity and personal development are integrated into its core strategy?

- What examples from companies like Google and Salesforce can be applied to your organization to build a culture that values growth, inclusivity, and social responsibility?

Epilogue
Embracing the People Dividend: A Roadmap to Sustainable Success

As I conclude this exploration into the transformative power of people-centered leadership, it is imperative to reflect on the vital themes and actionable strategies presented throughout this book. *The People Dividend: Leadership Strategies for Unlocking Employee Potential* is not merely a theoretical discourse; it is a loud and clear call for a paradigm shift in how organizations value and engage their most precious resource—people.

The Human-Centered Workplace: Redefining Leadership

In Chapter 1, we embarked on a journey to understand the essence and impact of humanistic management. Through historical perspectives and contemporary case studies, I highlighted the profound influence that people-centered leadership has on productivity, creativity, and employee satisfaction. The chapter underscored the significance of understanding employees as whole individuals rather than mere cogs in the corporate machine. This foundational concept set the stage for the subsequent discussions on respect, dignity, individualism, and inclusion.

Respect and Dignity: Building a Culture of Mutual Regard

Chapter 2 explored the bedrock principles of respect and dignity. These core values are essential in delivering a workplace culture where everyone feels valued and motivated. By examining the evolution of workplace culture and presenting convincing research findings, I made the business case for cultivating a respectful environment. The strategies for implementing a culture of respect are not just best practices but necessary steps toward achieving a harmonious and productive workplace.

Valuing Individuals and Individualism: Celebrating Uniqueness

Moving forward, Chapter 3 emphasized the importance of recognizing and valuing individual contributions. In an environment where standardization often overshadows individuality, this chapter highlighted the strategic imperative of personal development and the empowerment of individual talents. Through practical checklists and tools, leaders are equipped to acknowledge and harness the unique strengths of their team members, thereby driving engagement and performance.

Unlocking Potential through Diversity and Inclusion

Chapter 4 focused on the critical role of diversity and inclusion in unlocking an organization's full potential. I explored the innovation imperative and the necessity of cultivating an inclusive environment where diverse voices are empowered. By addressing common resistance and providing measurable frameworks for progress, I offered concrete steps for leaders to champion inclusion effectively. This chapter reinforced the idea that diversity is not just a moral obligation but a strategic advantage.

Beyond Production Elements – People at the Core

In Chapter 5, I discussed the shift from process-centric to people-centered leadership. By profiling transformation trailblazers and discussing the integration of psychological safety into organizational dynamics, I underscored the power of valuing people over processes. This chapter illustrated that when organizations prioritize their people, they spawn a culture of trust, innovation, and sustainable success.

Implementing Humanistic Values in Leadership

Chapter 7 provided a detailed roadmap for integrating humanistic values into leadership practices. It highlighted the practical steps leaders can take to embed these principles into their daily operations and strategic planning. By focusing on authenticity, empathy, and collaboration, leaders can drive meaningful change and cultivate a culture that consistently honors and uplifts its members.

The Future of Work with the People Dividend

Finally, Chapter 8 looked ahead to the future of work,

envisioning how organizations can continue to evolve by embracing the people dividend. It examined emerging trends, technological advancements, and social shifts that will shape the workplace of tomorrow. This chapter encouraged leaders to remain adaptable and forward-thinking, ensuring their commitment to human-centered principles remains steadfast amidst change.

The Path Forward: Sustained Commitment to Human-Centered Leadership

As I stand at the culmination of this comprehensive guide, it is clear that unlocking the people dividend requires sustained commitment and intentional action. The strategies and insights provided throughout this book are designed to inspire and equip leaders to create workplaces where every individual can thrive.

Practical Steps for Leaders

To ensure lasting impact, here are some practical steps for leaders:

1. **Engage in habitual learning**: Stay informed about the latest research and best practices in human-centered leadership. Attend workshops, read relevant literature, and engage with thought leaders in the field.

2. **Encourage open communication**: Create open and honest communication channels within your organization. Encourage feedback and be receptive to new ideas.

3. **Invest in personal development**: Provide opportunities for employees to grow and develop their skills. Support their career aspirations and recognize their achievements.

4. **Champion diversity and inclusion**: Actively promote diversity and inclusion initiatives. Ensure that all voices are heard and respected.

5. **Prioritize integrity**: Lead by example and uphold the highest standards of integrity. Build a culture of trust and accountability.

The Ripple Effect: Transforming Organizations and Communities

The impact of embracing the people dividend extends beyond the confines of individual organizations. When leaders commit to human-centered practices, they contribute to the broader goal of creating more equitable, inclusive, and thriving communities. The ripple effect of positive change can inspire other organizations and leaders to follow suit, creating a collective movement toward a more humane and sustainable future.

Final Thoughts

In conclusion, *The People Dividend: Leadership Strategies for Unlocking Employee Potential* offers a comprehensive and actionable framework for transforming leadership and organizational culture. By prioritizing respect, dignity, individualism, diversity, and integrity, leaders can unlock the full potential of their employees and achieve remarkable results.

As you implement these lessons and strategies, remember that the journey towards human-centered leadership is ongoing. It requires dedication, empathy, and a genuine commitment to valuing people. The rewards, however, are profound—not just in terms of organizational success but also in creating workplaces where every individual can flourish.

Thank you for embarking on this journey with me. Together, let us continue to unlock the people dividend and build a better, more inclusive future for all.

References

Preface

[1] Harter, J. (2023). *In new workplace, U.S. employee engagement stagnates.* Gallup. https://www.gallup.com/workplace/608675/new-workplace-employee-engagement-stagnates.aspx

[2] Bersin, J. (2023, November 26). *Companies have been neglecting their leadership, and it shows.* Josh Bersin. https://joshbersin.com/2023/11/companies-have-been-neglecting-their-leadership-and-it-shows/

[3] Feser, C., Mayol, F., & Srinivasan, R. (2014). Decoding leadership: What really matters. *McKinsey Quarterly* (4), 88-91. https://www.mckinsey.com/featured-insights/leadership/decoding-leadership-what-really-matters

[4] Feser, C., Nielsen, N., & Rennie, M. (2017). What's missing in leadership development? *McKinsey Quarterly* (3), 20-24.

[5] Tabrizi, B. (2015). 75% of cross-functional teams are dysfunctional. *Harvard Business Review.* https://hbr.org/2015/06/75-of-cross-functional-teams-are-dysfunctional

Chapter 1

[6] World Health Organization. (2024). *Depression.* WHO. https://www.who.int/health-topics/depression#tab=tab_1

[7] The Hubble Team. (2023). *The official list of every company's back-to-office strategy.* Hubble. https://hubblehq.com/blog/famous-companies-workplace-strategies

[8] Horne, M. (2021). *Integrity by design: Working and living authentically.* Pleasanton, CA: Boardwalk Research Press.

[9] Watson, T. (2012). *Global Workforce Study.* Employee Engagement. https://employeeengagement.com/wp-content/uploads/2012/11/2012-Towers-Watson-Global-Workforce-Study.pdf

[10] Navarra, K. (2023). *SHRM report underscores global importance of workplace culture.* SHRM. https://www.shrm.org/topics-tools/news/employee-relations/global-workplace-culture-research

[11] Deloitte. (2020). *2020 Global human capital trends report.* https://www2.deloitte.com/cn/en/pages/human-capital/articles/global-human-capital-trends-2020.html

[12] Edelman Trust Institute. (2024). *2024 Edelman trust barometer.* Edelman.

https://www.edelman.com/sites/g/files/aatuss191/fil
es/2024-
02/2024%20Edelman%20Trust%20Barometer%20
Global%20Report_FINAL.pdf

[13] Egan, N. W. (2017). *PEOPLE's 50 companies that care
2017.* Yahoo Entertainment.
https://www.yahoo.com/entertainment/peoples-50-
companies-care-2017-195301105.html

[14] SAS. (2023). *2023 SAS corporate social responsibility –
employees and culture.*
https://www.sas.com/content/dam/SAS/documents/
corporate-collateral/brochures/en-csr-employees-
culture-110855.pdf

[15] Semler, R. (2007). Out of this world: Doing things the
Semco way. *Global Business & Organizational
Excellence, 26*(5), 13-21.

[16] Miller, B. (2022). *How we inspire great performance at
Adobe.* Adobe Blog.
https://blog.adobe.com/en/publish/2022/05/09/how-
we-inspire-great-performance-at-adobe

[17] Alex Gorsky. (2024, March 9). In *Wikipedia.* Retrieved
July 5, 2024 from
https://en.wikipedia.org/wiki/Alex_Gorsky.

[18] Carnegie, M. (2023, February 23). *Tech's productivity
obsession is toxic.* Wired.
https://www.wired.com/story/techs-productivity-
obsession-is-toxic/

[19] McKendrick, J. (2024, March 29). *Technology's muddled impact on productivity.* Forbes. https://www.forbes.com/sites/joemckendrick/2024/03/29/technologys-muddled-impact-on-productivity/

[20] Sekar, N. (2024, June 27). *Google's "20% time" policy.* Medium. https://medium.com/@nareshnavinash/googles-20-time-policy-60d5706084be#.

Chapter 2

[21] Genentech. (2024). *Our promise.* https://www.gene.com/

[22] Semuels, A. (2023). *Now's the time to bring up menopause at work.* TIME. https://time.com/6290706/menopause-care-work-us-companies/

[23] Thomas, B., & Lucas, K. (2019). Development and validation of the workplace dignity scale. *Group & Organization Management, 44*(1), 72-111. https://doi.org/10.1177/1059601118807784

[24] Doheny, K. (2022). *Respect: How managers can deliver what workers want.* SHRM. https://www.shrm.org/topics-tools/news/managing-smart/respect-how-managers-can-deliver-workers-want

[25] Porath, C. (2014). Half of employees don't feel respected by their bosses. *Harvard Business Review.* https://hbr.org/2014/11/half-of-employees-dont-

feel-respected-by-their-bosses

[26] Gallup. (2023). *The benefits of employee engagement.* https://www.gallup.com/workplace/236927/employee-engagement-drives-growth.aspx

[27] Dixon-Fyle, S., Dolan, K., Hunt, V., & Prince, S. (2020). Diversity wins: How inclusion matters. *McKinsey Insights.*

[28] Dixon-Fyle, S., Huber, C., Márquez, M. d. M. M., Prince, S., Thomas, A., & Hunt, V. (2023). Diversity matters even more: The case for holistic impact. *McKinsey Insights.*

[29] Rogers, K. (2018, July-August). Do your employees feel respected? *Harvard Business Review.* https://hbr.org/2018/07/do-your-employees-feel-respected

[30] Brown, T. (2021). *The questions every corporate innovation leader asks about culture, answered.* Sifted. https://sifted.eu/articles/culture-change-common-questions

[31] Ben & Jerry's Homemade, Inc. (2024). https://www.benjerry.com/

[32] Microsoft. (2024). *Global diversity and inclusion.* https://www.microsoft.com/en-us/diversity/default

[33] Salesforce, Inc. (2024). *Let's build a more inclusive workplace and world.*

https://www.salesforce.com/company/equality/

[34] WWF. (2024). *Diversity, equity, and inclusion at WWF.*
https://www.worldwildlife.org/pages/deij-at-wwf

[35] Patagonia, Inc. (2024). *Everything we make has an impact on the planet.*
https://www.patagonia.com/our-footprint/

[36] Formula for change. (2024, January 5). In *Wikipedia.*
Retrieved July 6, 2024 from
https://en.wikipedia.org/wiki/Formula_for_change

[37] Mautz, S. (2019, December 9). *Tim Cook powerfully expressed the importance of showing respect. Here are 9 ways to show employees more of it.* Inc.
https://www.inc.com/scott-mautz/tim-cook-powerfully-expressed-importance-of-showing-respect-here-are-9-ways-to-show-employees-more-of-it.html

Chapter 3

[38] Edmondson, A.C. (2019). *The fearless organization: Creating psychological safety in the workplace for learning, innovation, and growth.* John Wiley & Sons, Inc.

[39] Hill, L. (2022). Leaders must engage with emotions as never before: The role of emotional intelligence in driving effective change. Harvard Business Review. Retrieved from https://hbr.org/2022/01/leaders-must-engage-with-emotions-as-never-before

[40] Johnson, S., & Blanchard, K. H. (1982). *The one minute manager.* New York: Morrow.

[41] Rigoni, B., & Asplund, J. (2016). *Strengths-based employee development: The business results.* Gallup. https://www.gallup.com/workplace/236297/strengths-based-employee-development-business-results.aspx

[42] Dweck, C. S. (2006). *Mindset: The new psychology of success.* New York, NY: Random House.

[43] Medtronic, Inc. (2024). *Engineering the extraordinary.* https://europe.medtronic.com/xd-en/index.html

[44] Makoto, M. (2019). Empowerment through self-improvement skills: The role of learning goals and personal growth initiative. Journal of Vocational Behavior, 115. Retrieved August 20, 2024, from https://www.sciencedirect.com/science/article/abs/pii/S0001879119300697?via%3Dihub

[45] Bourke, J., & Garr, S. (2017). *Diversity and inclusion: The reality gap.* Deloitte. https://www.deloitte.com/global/en/our-thinking/insights/topics/talent/human-capital-trends/diversity-and-inclusion-at-the-workplace.html

Chapter 4

[46] Myers, V. (2015). *Diversity is being invited to the party:*

Inclusion is being asked to dance. [Video].
YouTube.
https://www.youtube.com/watch?v=9gS2VPUkB3
M

[47] Darden Concepts, Inc. (2024). *About us.* Retrieved
August 20, 2024, from
https://www.darden.com/our-company

[48] Intel Corporation. (2024). *Diversity and inclusion are key
to innovation.* Intel.
https://www.intel.com/content/www/us/en/diversity
/diversity-at-intel.html

[49] Target Brands, Inc. (2024). *Diversity, equity and
inclusion.* Target. Retrieved August 20, 2024, from
https://corporate.target.com/sustainability-
governance/our-team/diversity-equity-inclusion

[50] Starbucks Corporation. (2024). *Expect more than coffee.*
Retrieved August 20, 2024, from
https://careers.starbucks.com/culture/

[51] Walmart, Inc. (2024). *Belonging, diversity, equity and
inclusion report.* Retrieved August 20, 2024, from
https://corporate.walmart.com/purpose/belonging-
diversity-equity-inclusion/belonging-diversity-
equity-and-inclusion-report

[52] Boston Scientific Corporation. (2024). *Diversity, equity,
and inclusion.* Boston Scientific. Retrieved August
20, 2024, from
https://www.bostonscientific.com/en-

US/careers/working-here/diversity-and-
inclusion.html

Chapter 5

[53] Morvaridi, B. (Ed.) (2015). *New Philanthropy and social
justice: Debating the conceptual and policy
discourse.* Cambridge University Press.

[54] PR Newswire. (2024, April 29). *AMD's Dr. Lisa Su
named* Chief Executive Magazine's *2024 CEO of
the Year.* https://www.prnewswire.com/news-
releases/amds-dr-lisa-su-named-chief-executive-
magazines-2024-ceo-of-the-year-302129268.html

[55] Bunkley, N. (2017). GM's crusade: Transforming work
culture. *Automotive News, 91.*

[56] Nooyi, I. (2019). Profit and purpose: Indra Nooyi, former
PepsiCo chairman, talks about balancing bottom
line and societal success. *Directors & Boards,
43*(2), 18-20.

[57] Liberty Mind. (2022). *Zappos – The culture everyone
wants to copy.* https://libertymind.co.uk/zappos-the-
culture-everyone-wants-to-copy/

[58] Nine to Five. (2019). *How Spotify keeps its culture social
and fresh.* Medium.
https://medium.com/@info_37650/how-spotify-
keeps-its-culture-social-and-fresh-de4b8e0fb222

[59] Gregory, L. (2023). *Unilever's organizational culture &*

cultural traits. Panmore Institute.
https://panmore.com/unilever-organizational-
culture-of-performance

[60] Edmondson, A.C. (2019). *The fearless organization: Creating psychological safety in the workplace for learning, innovation, and growth.* John Wiley & Sons, Inc.

Chapter 6

[61] Tayan, B. (2019). *The Wells Fargo cross-selling scandal.* Harvard Law School Forum on Corporate Governance.
https://corpgov.law.harvard.edu/2019/02/06/the-wells-fargo-cross-selling-scandal-2/

[62] LRN Corporation. (2024, May 13). *New LRN research: Gen Z employees twice as likely to bend the rules or engage in workplace misconduct.* LRN.
https://blog.lrn.com/lrn-research-finds-growing-focus-on-ai-incentives-and-accountability-mechanisms-0

[63] The Arbinger Institute. (2002). *Leadership and self-deception: Getting out of the box.* Berrett-Koehler Publishers.

[64] Neff, K. (2011). *Self-compassion: The proven power of being kind to yourself.* HarperCollins e-books.

Chapter 7

[65] Sinek, S. (2014). *Leaders eat last: Why some teams pull together and others don't.* New York, New York: Portfolio.

[66] Csikszentmihalyi, M. (2014). *Flow and the foundations of positive psychology: The collected works of Mihaly Csikszentmihalyi.* Berlin: Springer.

Chapter 8

[67] U.S. Senate Sergeant at Arms. (2022, March 13). *NEWS: Sanders introduces legislation to enact a 32-hour workweek with no loss in pay.* Retrieved August 20, 2024, from https://www.sanders.senate.gov/press-releases/news-sanders-introduces-legislation-to-enact-a-32-hour-workweek-with-no-loss-in-pay/

[68] Lau, V., & Sigurdardottir, R. (2021, October 14). The shorter work week really worked in Iceland. Here's how. *Time Magazine.* https://time.com/6106962/shorter-work-week-iceland/

[69] McCarthy, J. (2023). *Round-up of Gallup Covid-19 coverage.* Gallup. https://news.gallup.com/opinion/gallup/308126/roundup-gallup-covid-coverage.aspx

[70] Global Workplace Analytics. (2024). *Telework savings potential.* https://globalworkplaceanalytics.com/cut-oil

Index

About The Author

Mike Horne, Ph.D., is a highly experienced global corporate human resources and organization development leader, distinguished executive coach, best-selling author, and sought-after speaker. He is dedicated to empowering aspiring leaders, executives, and teams to navigate transitions, excel in new roles, and increase their effectiveness and influence.

Since launching his coaching career in 2018, Dr. Horne has guided numerous leaders and teams in adopting goal-directed behaviors that create immediate improvements and long-term behavioral changes that sustain progress. Presently, he collaborates with industry leaders in biopharmaceuticals, technology, professional services, finance, and medical devices, among others. Dr. Horne hosts *The People Dividend Podcast*, a platform where meaningful dialogue, diverse perspectives, and inspiring stories come together to redefine the world of human capital. It currently ranks in the top 10% of all podcasts globally.

Previously, for nearly three decades, Dr. Horne held pivotal human resources and organization development roles, including the head of Human Resources for Gilead Sciences' research division, global leader of Talent and Development for Brocade, and head of Organization Development for Genentech. Before these positions, he served for fifteen years in human resources leadership roles for Nortel Networks, Marriott International, Willis Towers

Watson, and the National Labor Relations Board.

His current book, *The People Dividend: Leadership Strategies for Unlocking Potential,* describes the return on investment businesses experience through investing in their employees' growth and well-being. He highlights key areas for investment, including building trust, encouraging motivation, ensuring open communication, retaining employees, making better decisions, and enhancing the organization's reputation. He is also the author of *Integrity by Design: Working and Living Authentically,* which calls readers to their higher purpose and inspires them to work and live authentically.

Dr. Horne is the graduate faculty chair of Human Resources Management and Leadership at Golden Gate University (San Francisco). He holds multiple coaching credentials, including Immunity to Change and Positive Intelligence Coaching. He has provided strategic guidance to the American Foundation for the Blind and the American National Red Cross. Dr. Horne is a returned Peace Corps Volunteer (Solomon Islands).

Dr. Horne earned his Ph.D. in Human and Organization Development from Fielding Graduate Institute. He received a Master's in Human Resources and Organization Development from American University and a Bachelor of Science in Labor Relations from La Salle University.

You can contact Dr. Horne via his website, email, and phone number given below:

URL: mike-horne.com

Contact number: +1 760-636-4411

Email: info@mike-horne.com

26020425R00146